# PRESENT!

## A TECHIE'S GUIDE TO PUBLIC SPEAKING

by Poornima Vijayashanker and Karen Catlin

D1042490

Designer: Pauly Ting
Cover: Anton Khodakovsky
Editor: Nathalie Arbel

Femgineer
Palo Alto, California
http://www.femgineer.com

# DEDICATION

To voices that deserve to be heard for their experiences and ideas, and to talent that deserves to be showcased for a more diverse and inclusive tech industry.

# TABLE OF CONTENTS

# FOREWORD

By Jennifer Dulski, President and COO of Change.org

I became comfortable with public speaking in an unusual setting before my tech career started, having earned my stripes as a high school teacher in my early twenties. It was quite nerve-racking, especially at first, because every day I had to come prepared to talk about a new topic – and all in front of an audience. Granted, my audience was made up entirely of teenagers, but teenagers are among the most judgmental (or at least the most awkward) audiences. When I taught ninth-grade Health, and had to face "anonymous question box day" with uncomfortable questions about bodies and sex, I knew that nearly any speech I would give after that would seem easy in comparison.

I now speak regularly as part of my work, and whether they are small "fireside chats" or keynotes in front of thousands of people, the opportunities to speak have led to many great outcomes. I've been able to increase awareness and action around causes I care about, form new partnerships, and hire great people.

While I gain so much value from public speaking, I have also had my fair share of "learning the hard way" experiences as well. From technical glitches with slides to being interviewed by someone who held the one available microphone less than an inch away from my mouth for an entire interview, I know that tips like the ones in this book would have served me well as I headed into those talks.

At their best, great talks inspire people. I've been inspired by a wide array of speakers, from Guy Kawasaki presenting tips for startup founders to Brené Brown's incredibly self-aware TED talk on the power of vulnerability. And what I've learned is that the most moving talks often have stories at their center. I am lucky to be able to tell the incredible stories of our petition starters at Change.org, like Laxmi, who helped prevent acid attacks on women in India, or Elena, who made school textbooks more affordable for families in Spain. Their stories are a gift to me as a speaker, and I hope that by telling their stories, my speaking can be a gift to them too.

Poornima Vijayashanker and Karen Catlin have written an excellent book to help you find the stories worth telling. Whether you are just getting started or working to hone your craft as a speaker, you'll find practical tips and hands-on exercises for all stages of the public speaking process, from planning to practicing to pitching and more. And, while the book is primarily aimed at people working in tech, the tips they include are relevant for people in virtually any industry who want to share their expertise with others and grow their careers through public speaking.

I first met Karen through her husband, who is our VP of Engineering at Change.org. When Karen told me about her professional focus of advocating for women in the tech industry, I asked her to help us with our efforts to improve gender diversity and create a welcoming environment for technical women in particular. Karen identified things we could do to recruit and retain female employees and encouraged me to speak more in public about being a leader in tech. Through public speaking, not only would I recruit more candidates to Change.org, but, as Karen pointed out, I would also inspire other women who are seeking role models in the tech industry.

Karen introduced us to Poornima, and we hosted her Femgineer Forum at our San Francisco headquarters. Poornima's approach to educating, encouraging, and empowering women resonated with us and our goal to improve gender diversity.

Poornima and Karen are both accomplished technologists, with experience giving talks around the world at conferences, universities, and leading tech companies. In their book, they share the lessons they've learned to put others on the fast track to becoming successful public speakers. They weave in real-life examples and stories about developing skills that will lead to career opportunities, and detailed exercises to make practicing easier.

The authors are role models for anyone who wants to do more public speaking. And they are role models for women. As the tech industry is coming to understand that diversity is good for business, it's critical for more women to speak about their work at conferences and industry events. Too often throughout my career, I have been the sole woman on the stage, and I am grateful for Karen and Poornima's efforts to change that.

I know you all have powerful stories and ideas to share with the world, so I hope you will take inspiration from this book, and I look forward to seeing you onstage!

- Jennifer Dulski

# ACKNOWLEDGMENTS

We deeply appreciate the following people for devoting time to reading our manuscript, providing detailed feedback, and keeping us motivated to get it out the door:

Angus Mark

Anna Liu

Anuradha Sridharan

Cate Huston

Emily Leathers

Emma Catlin

Jennifer Zaczek

Judith Coley

Kate Hammer

Kitt Hodsden

Lucy Spencer

Mary Ann Walsh

Molly Inglish

Poonam Dhidlyali

Roy Chong

We're grateful for Jen Dulski, who wrote a heartfelt and inspiring foreword to our book.

We're thankful to the following companies for partnering with us to make a positive impact in the tech industry by sponsoring the production of this book:

**Platinum Sponsors**
Intuit
Orate

**Gold Sponsors**
Altera
Frankly
Pinterest

**Partners**
Publishizer

We'd like to recognize and thank the following people as patrons who cared so deeply about us and about bringing this book to life that they chose to make a personal investment in its production.

Alex Notov

Andrew Mills

Carolina Salas

Charlie Cardin

Diana Espino

Guy Vincent

Marcus Eagan

Ron Wilson

Sthir Malkpar

Tim, Emma, and Ted Catlin

Thanks to our skilled and always encouraging editor, Nathalie Arbel. Nathalie provided us with an endless source of support along with the gentle nudges we needed throughout the process to take this book to a level we are both extremely proud of.

Thanks to our talented and devoted designer, Pauly Ting, for transforming our words into a beautiful book.

Thanks to our kindhearted video editor, Gary Kirk, who was instrumental in creating the audio and video portions of the interactive bundle.

Last but not least, we want to thank the people we share our lives with for their support while we were working on this book, and for cheering us on every time we speak in public. Aaron, Tim, Emma, Ted, and Judy, we couldn't do what we do without you!

# INTRODUCTION

To grow your career, you know what you need to do: improve your public speaking skills.

Public speaking provides the visibility and professional credibility that helps you score the next big opportunity and build important relationships with members of your field.

But even more important is the fact that it transforms the way you communicate. Improved confidence and the ability to convey messages clearly will impact your relationships with your managers, coworkers, customers, and industry peers.

And let's face it. Without making your work visible through effective communication, you'll be overlooked. It happens to many of us: a promotion denied, feeling stuck in our careers, or being frustrated when others are recognized instead of us, even if we work just as hard as they do.

When we realized we should speak in public, we took the plunge and started giving talks in the tech community. Were we nervous? Sure. Did we make mistakes along the way? Absolutely. But we stuck with it, and we are now confident presenters who regularly give talks at conferences, corporate events, and public speaking workshops.

Even though it's scary, public speaking is the best way to leap to the next level in your career. We believe everyone can develop great public speaking skills, and we're living proof.

## Why we wrote this book

We have two simple goals.

Our first is to share with you what works for us and the students we've coached. As techies, we've spent decades presenting abstract and complex concepts to employees, teammates, bosses, and customers, and we've learned what engages audiences and what causes them to tune out. This guide gives you our tried-and-true techniques and puts you on the fast track to becoming a successful public speaker. Besides, we have some embarrassing stories that are just too good to keep to ourselves.

Our second goal is to see more people speak. We believe in making the tech world more inclusive, and part of that mission is to encourage you to share your expertise. We want to bring life to more voices that might be silenced by fear and self-doubt or are simply left out of the conversation.

## Who we are and how public speaking transformed us

We're Poornima Vijayashanker and Karen Catlin, and we've built our careers around our love for public speaking. We regularly give talks around the world, from in-house corporate presentations to conference keynotes and panels. We also teach: we've coached hundreds of people in the art and science of effective communication, including startup founders, employees at Fortune 500s, and emerging experts in tech fields.

Both of us have engineering backgrounds. We weren't born public speakers, and at first we experienced so much stage fright that we were reluctant to get up in front of crowds. But once we learned how to speak in public, we didn't want to stop.

Karen caught the speaking bug thanks to a mentor.

 *It all started when I avoided her question. A mentor and I were walking in the hills above Stanford University, and I wanted her advice on how to build my new leadership coaching practice. It was going well until she asked whether I enjoyed public speaking. Before answering, I took a deep breath and felt my heart start to race. You see, I had done some public speaking before, but not that much. The thought of having to do more of it made me nervous - really nervous. But I already knew, deep down inside, that I needed to become a more active public speaker. It would be the key to building my new brand and getting the word out about my coaching business. I also knew that this mentor could connect me with speaking opportunities. So I avoided her question and instead responded, "I need to do more of it."*

*Soon afterward, I set a goal for myself: to speak in public at least once every month. That was in 2012, and I am proud to say that I have given dozens of talks since then. Most months I give at least one presentation, and at my busiest I've spoken five times in one month. I've presented at conferences, at tech companies across Silicon Valley, and at universities. I've even given a TEDx talk.[1]*

*Because I forced myself to speak in public every month, I'm now a confident public speaker who rarely gets nervous. If my mentor were to ask me again, "Do you* enjoy public speaking," I'd answer, "Absolutely! Do you have an event in mind?"

Poornima went from being a shy kid to a confident presenter.

 *I wasn't born a social butterfly. In fact, I was pretty shy and self-conscious.*

*During the most awkward years of my life, I decided to take the plunge and put myself out there. Was I scared? You bet! I started speaking in public when I was twelve. Yup, I was one of those speech and debate geeks in middle school and high school.*

*Public speaking at such a young age helped me come out of my shell and taught me how to communicate my ideas clearly and confidently. It took lots of practice and coaching, but I got there.*

*I attribute almost every success and happy memory I've had since my middle school days to my public speaking abilities:*

- *Getting through my college interview and being accepted to Duke*
- *Nailing my first technical job interview in Silicon Valley*
- *Raising capital from investors*
- *Delivering my first TEDx talk onstage [2]*
- *Officiating my best friend's wedding*

*Public speaking has brought me hundreds of opportunities, and I love helping others become confident presenters to unlock the opportunities in their own lives.*

## "Is this book for me?"

This book is for you if you want to improve your ability to communicate ideas, no matter how technical or complex.

Public speaking helps people in many roles - engineers, product managers, online marketers, designers, startup founders, and tech entrepreneurs. The techniques here work for people of all levels, from junior employees to senior experts in a field.

No matter where you are in your career, you'll come across opportunities to give presentations. Sometimes these presentations are required for your job, or they might be extracurricular. These are some examples of public speaking:

- Showcasing a project to your teammates or upper management at work
- Presenting your product to potential customers or current clients
- Delivering a tech talk at your company
- Giving a talk or even the keynote speech at a major industry conference

Our students often express concern that they don't feel eligible to be public speakers and that they don't have anything to say.

We believe that generosity is the root of excellent public speaking. When you get down to it, when you give a presentation, you help your audience by sharing your knowledge, expertise, and anecdotes.

If you adopt this viewpoint, you'll see that your experiences are valuable to others and you'll become confident that you are more than qualified to speak up. You'll also find that giving a presentation from a place of goodwill is very fulfilling.

And you don't have to give one talk per month like Karen did. If you're just getting started, you can take small steps like explaining something in a meeting.

## How to use this guide

This book is a guide to help you build a talk from scratch and deliver it professionally, and each chapter leads you through one step in the process.

Our process works for a wide range of common presentation formats in tech and is also applicable to many scenarios where you need to communicate clearly, whether it's to your work team, customers, or even hundreds and thousands of people in a conference hall.

It took us years of trial and error to get to where we are, and the chapters that follow are jam-packed with our personal stories, stories from our students, and activities to apply what you've learned.

If you're new to public speaking (or have a speaking slot but no talk yet), treat this book like a recipe. If you've cooked anything before, you know that missing an ingredient or skipping a step can result in disaster, or at least wasted time. Start from the beginning and try each activity before progressing to the next one. By the end, you'll have a finished presentation and will be prepared to present with confidence.

If you've been speaking for a while and want to focus on developing specific skills, or need a crash course on a specific topic right away (e.g., you're already scheduled to give a talk at a conference in a few days and need tips for handling Q&A), feel free to skip to a specific chapter. Just be aware that many activities build on one another, so you may have to refer to earlier chapters for context.

Take the time to put the activities into practice. This will solidify what you learned in a chapter and is a fast way to bring your talk to life.

Most of us are unaware of how we really present, and awareness is the key to real improvement. Therefore, we'll ask you to record yourself speaking in several activities. You'll notice your speech patterns and body movements when you watch your recordings, and this helps you adopt behaviors that improve your presentation style and autocorrect ones that detract. For example, you'll learn which tone of voice makes you sound conversational or reduce hand movements that distract from what you're saying. Recording also acts as a forcing function to get you to complete the exercise. Many of our students are initially reluctant to do it, but they realize the value when they notice their quick progress.

For easier planning, we've also marked activities that involve the help of one or more friends. Practicing in front of friends or coworkers is the best way to simulate the conditions and emotions you'll encounter during a real presentation. They can also offer helpful feedback and make the process more fun.

Visit the ★ Present! interactive bundle online (www.femgineer.com/present-book/interactive-bundle) to access all of the book's references, as well as pictures and videos that demonstrate techniques. After all, public speaking is a visual and auditory art.

Our tried-and-true methods will dramatically improve your speaking skills, but they take time and commitment. If you stick with them, you'll be on the fast track to presenting confidently. If you're just getting started, it may take six to twelve months of practice to become a confident speaker – and of course, we encourage you to keep practicing for the rest of your career so you get better and better.

Part I, Get in the Speaker State of Mind, explains how being a public speaker impacts your entire career. You'll also learn how to look at presentations as conversations.

Part II, Create Your Talk, is a step-by-step process to create a talk from scratch. Use it whenever you need to develop a brand-new talk, even if you don't have a topic yet; we'll show you how to find the pearls of wisdom and engaging stories hidden in your past. You'll end up with a practiced presentation and a proposal to get you accepted into speaking events.

Part III, Deliver Like a Pro, helps you convey your content in an engaging, clear, and confident way. You'll learn how to combat stage fright (which is common among both inexperienced and experienced public speakers), use your body and voice, and accent your talk with slides.

Part IV, The Finishing Touches, helps prepare you for the day of your talk. You'll learn how to finesse Q&A sessions, handle tough audiences, and take care of some details the day before your talk to make sure everything goes smoothly. You'll also learn how to promote your talk to reach more people.

Part V, Special Talk Formats, explains how to adapt your presentation for formats that are common in the tech world, yet differ structurally. You'll learn about lightning talks, long-form talks, and panels and you'll also learn how to use the web to deliver presentations online and increase the reach of any talk you deliver.

We've also included a bonus chapter, Become a Meeting Maven. We consider meetings to be public speaking, even if they're with people you see every day, and many of us start our public speaking careers in these work environments. We'll show you how public speaking techniques help you convey information clearly and excel in common workplace situations.

You'll get tips on how to present at meetings and learn how to make requests that get approved, whether you're asking your manager for vacation time or convincing your team to undergo a multi-million-dollar initiative.

## What this book doesn't cover

This book won't teach you how to pitch a startup idea to investors, how to give a product demo, or how to negotiate. You can certainly apply our techniques to improve your game; however, we don't focus on those areas.

Public speaking can be a source of income, and getting paid to speak is an advanced topic that we don't cover here. Consider checking out the Femgineer Confident Communicator Course,[3] which teaches you how to go from making $0 to up to five figures per talk.

## Don't hold back

Before we jump in, let's talk about three objections that might hold you back from making real progress. They come up for our students all the time.

- *"I'm not cut out for this."*
  We're here to tell you that you are cut out for it. None of us were good at public speaking when we started. As long as you put in the time, try our recommended techniques and exercises progressively, and practice, you will improve. You'll surprise yourself with your confidence and presentation know-how.

- *"Been there, done that."*

If you've done any speaking before, you might say to yourself, "I already know this..."

It might be tempting to skip over a section. But often we don't put our knowledge into practice. A refresher course can force us to try a technique in real life rather than keeping it locked up in our minds.

So when you think, "I already know this," stop and ask yourself, "Is there something new here I haven't tried?" And then ask, "Am I actually putting this into practice?"

- *"This technique doesn't apply to me."*
  You might read one of our suggestions and say to yourself, "This won't work for me..."

A little outside perspective can help in these situations. If you're stuck, we can suggest a tweak that makes a technique more effective for you. Contact us via Twitter @femgineer[4] or search for #presentbook.[5]

Are you ready? Let's go.

# PART I

## GET IN THE SPEAKER STATE OF MIND

---

Let's get started with your public speaking journey in Chapter 1 by looking at why public speaking gives careers a boost. We know from our own experience and the track records of our students that public speaking is a worthwhile investment, which is why we're so passionate about teaching it.

Chapter 2 helps you mentally frame a talk as a conversation. This mindset is a good one to adopt early on, before you even start creating a presentation, because it takes the pressure off and reduces anxiety around "performing well." It also helps you practice and maintain a relaxed tone that people will respond well to.

Once you're in this state of mind, you'll do your first activity: creating a short recording of yourself talking about a fun, conversational topic. We'll build on this activity later, so make sure you take a little time to practice recording yourself.

# 1

# GET READY TO TRANSFORM YOUR CAREER

Public speaking is like a career multivitamin with many benefits. Here are five noticeable changes that public speaking brings.

## Doors will open

Public speaking creates opportunities.

If you're an employee at a company, speaking is a chance to show off your achievements confidently and attract sponsors who will champion your efforts and goals. People will take notice of your expertise when you present a recent project at an internal event or speak confidently and clearly in a meeting. This is important if you tend to be "heads down" and rarely promote your work.

If you're looking for your next job, then presenting at a conference is a great way for you to show off your expertise and get hired. And if you're an entrepreneur, speaking at pitch events helps you get in front of notable investors, while conferences give you a chance to spread the word about your products to potential customers.

As coaches and entrepreneurs, we've encountered opportunities including consulting engagements, new professional connections, more speaking gigs, and projects that make an impact in the community.

## Networking will become easier

If you learn how to give a talk with confidence, you'll become more comfortable talking in front of people in general. You'll improve your presence and ability to convey your ideas more clearly, whether you're connecting with attendees at events, colleagues at work, or new friends you just met at your local coffee shop. In addition, knowing you have something valuable to discuss makes networking easier. (The first step in preparing your talk is to find helpful experiences and lessons that you can contribute to the world, as you'll see in Chapter 3.)

When you're a speaker at a specific event, you benefit in a different way than you do if you are an attendee. Even though events and conferences are prime networking grounds, it can be difficult to know who are the right people to connect with – ones who share your interests or need your expertise. You may also feel intimidated when approaching strangers.

But when you're a speaker at an event, the right people approach you.

People self-select based on the topic you spoke about, so they're likely to have similar interests. In our experiences, after we've given great talks, people have asked us insightful questions and offered ideas and opportunities. Those conversations are more useful than ones we might have in a hallway or bar as an attendee. It's not just small talk; it's substantive.

This effect extends beyond an event you spoke at. If you re-purpose your presentation for distribution on the web, you can connect with people from all around the world long after you've given your talk.

## You'll attract top talent

If you're a startup founder or a hiring manager at a tech company, you know that filling open positions is a challenge because of the limited talent supply.

Public speaking is a great hiring tool because it helps people with similar interests find you, and it shows the face and personality of your company. A presentation is one of the most effective sales pitches.

 *Nearly 99 percent of my startup hires have resulted from talks I've given at events and conferences. It doesn't matter whether my talk was technical or business-related; potential hires approach me afterward. They're curious to hear what I'm working on, where I work, and whether there are any job opportunities.*

## You'll build your personal brand, both online and off

When you give a presentation, you're in a position of authority. Speakers are viewed as experts, and if you give high-quality talks, your credibility and reputation will improve.

You can also leverage your live speaking gigs to build a strong online presence. Promote or distribute your presentation content in blog posts, SlideShare, social media, and LinkedIn. (We'll teach you how to do this in Chapter 15.)

## You'll learn how to ask for what you want at work – and get it

The root of good public speaking skills is the ability to clearly communicate information, and this comes in handy when you're making requests at work, big or small. The bonus chapter, Become a Meeting Maven, teaches you how to present requests in a

---

convincing and professional manner.

Can you see why improving this one skill – public speaking – gives you a leg up in your career?

# RECAP

## CHAPTER 1

**Public speaking packs a punch.**

Public speaking may seem like just one professional skill, but it will supercharge many areas of your career:

- Opportunities will find you.
- Networking will become easier.
- You'll attract top talent for your projects or company.
- You'll build your personal brand at work and online.
- You'll learn how to make requests that get approved.

# 2
# KEEP IT CONVERSATIONAL

Public speaking is not just for people who are natural performers. Nor is it reserved for executives and extroverts.

The benefits of public speaking are accessible to everyone, including you. It's a skill to learn, and in this chapter, we'll take the first baby step: to get in the mindset that a talk is like a conversation.

If you stay conversational, you'll be more comfortable with the idea of public speaking in general and come across as a confident presenter when you give talks.

## A conversation is an exchange of information

A well-laid-out conversation is an exchange of information. One person talks, the other listens. The listener may interject to ask a question or share their thoughts, followed by a response by the original speaker.

When you prepare a talk, think of it as an opportunity to convey valuable knowledge or entertain with your experiences and stories.

Imagine one person sitting with you to have a conversation about your talk topic and think about what they might like to learn. This gets you out of the mindset that a talk is all about you on a stage, distant from your audience, and puts you into the shoes of an audience member.

## A conversational mindset affects your tone

When you speak in a conversational tone, you're relaxed. You care about engaging the other person, and the goal is to be understood and to connect.

But when it's time to speak in public, people can forget that they're still just having a conversation. They're no longer speaking one-on-one, so they think they need to be formal. The presentation sounds forced and the listener immediately disconnects.

One way to sound formal or forced is to talk at your audience and command them to do something. Think of when your parents said, "Clean your room!" or lectured you about doing homework. You probably tuned out. In a similar vein, you'll cause a disconnect if you sound patronizing or overly pedantic by talking to the audience as if they "don't know any better." Recall a professor or a teacher who made you feel stupid.

Forced formality also can manifest in strange ways through your voice and body language. You can become monotonous or overly exuberant without even realizing it. You can detect this by watching recordings of yourself speaking or asking for peer feedback. Another tip-off that you're being too formal is when you use a lot of industry jargon or words that a regular person wouldn't use.

Here's an activity to help you practice your conversational speech muscles while in a public speaking mindset. As the first activity of the book, it gets your feet wet in a safe setting and acts as a forcing function to transition you from reading about public speaking to doing it.

You'll be recording yourself, which helps you complete an activity in full and lets you see your speech and body language patterns that may previously have gone unnoticed. Make sure to try it because we'll be building on this activity in other chapters – and it's fun, especially if you have a sweet tooth!

# PRACTICE
## YOUR FAVORITE DESSERT

Practice a conversational speaking style by talking about your favorite dessert for two minutes. Make sure to record it so you can watch it and observe your tone.

1. **Prepare a recording device**
   You can use your phone or the camera on your computer with a recording service like Mac's Photo Booth.

2. **Pick your favorite dessert**
   It can be anything. Poornima's is ice cream, as you can see in the example video in the ★*Present!* interactive bundle under Chapter 2.

3. **Think about why you like it**
   You can do this in your head or jot down points on paper. Why do you like this dessert the most? Take a stance: Why is it better than every other dessert?

# PRACTICE CONTINUED

4. **Record yourself speaking for two minutes**
   Talk about your dessert and why you like it. In addition to sharing your reasons, think about how you can convey your enthusiasm with your tone, add a little humor, or share a short story. To help this feel natural, imagine that you're talking to a friend.

5. **Observe how the exercise feels and watch your recording**
   Did you feel at ease and comfortable? Did you sound conversational on the recording? If not, how might you do it differently?

## Sample recording

Check out a short video of Poornima talking about her favorite flavor of ice cream, Mexican chocolate, in the *Present!* interactive bundle. It's just a rough cut, nothing fancy.

# RECAP

## CHAPTER 2

### A talk is an exchange of information, like a conversation

- Imagine having a conversation with an audience member about a topic that benefits and entertains them.

- This helps you keep the audience in mind as you craft your talk. It also affects delivery; presenting with a conversational tone helps you connect with your audience.

# PART II

## CREATE YOUR TALK

Time to dive in. In Part II, you'll go through the process of creating a talk. We'll take you from "I have no idea what to speak about" to a fully developed presentation and proposal that you can submit to a conference.

Our process helps you avoid situations like this one.

 *In the summer of 2014, I was attending my first team retreat as an Entrepreneur-in-Residence at 500 Startups.*

*I wasn't sure what the format of the retreat would be, but the day before it began, one of my colleagues told me that usually people give presentations to their colleagues to pitch ideas they have for improvements to the accelerator. He suggested that I present on an idea he and I had been discussing recently.*

*This seemed like a great way to gauge interest and hopefully get buy in for our idea, but my gut was telling me that I hadn't spent enough time putting a presentation together.*

*I told my gut to shut up!*

*I asked for a slot the day of the retreat and got a fifteen-minute speaking opportunity not long before the presentation was about to begin. I only had about thirty minutes to prepare my slides and no time to rehearse what I was actually going to say.*

*When I got up to present, the slides didn't show up on the projector, and it took five minutes to fix them. I started to run through my presentation quickly because I only had ten minutes left.*

*When my time was up, everyone in the audience had quizzical looks on their faces. My presentation was haphazard and wasn't compelling and I felt very unprofessional.*

*People bombarded me with questions that I hadn't thought about, and by the end of the fifteen minutes I was ready to run out the door. There was no way my idea was going to be approved because my presentation was so far from being polished and thoughtful.*

Poornima's story shows that no matter how experienced you are or how confident you sound, a presentation that hasn't been thoughtfully prepared will fail to convey its main messages and incite action.

In this instance, she overlooked some key elements of preparation that make for a great talk:

- Ask about the format of an event in advance
- Think about the audience's takeaways
- Anticipate audience questions
- Practice alone and in front of other people
- Test slides before the presentation begins

We're about to share our tried-and-true method for creating a presentation that gets your message across clearly. You can start from zero and follow the chapters in Part II (in order, because they build on one another) to end up with a robust talk.

You'll first find a topic and stories to share (Chapters 3, 4, and 5). Then you'll create a professional proposal to submit to event organizers, and we'll show you exactly how to find speaking opportunities and what to write to organizers in an email when you approach them (Chapter 6). Finally, you'll develop your topic and proposal into a full presentation and practice it, incorporating peer feedback (Chapters 7 and 8).

We'll give you a general process that can apply to any length of talk. If you're developing a presentation for a specific format, like a lightning talk, long-form talk (over thirty minutes), panel, or webinar, we've included tips in Part V.

# 3
## FIND A TOPIC

The first step in creating a talk is to find a topic you can comfortably speak about and confirm that people find it interesting.

Think you don't have anything to present? Oh yes, you do. Remember: generosity is the root of excellent public speaking. You're sharing your experiences and perspectives with the audience to offer lessons learned, shortcuts, insights, and empathy.

Let's step back and take a look at your work to root out the gems that will create a helpful presentation.

### Yes, you're qualified to give a talk

You may be thinking, "Why would anyone care about what I have to say?"

Or, "What would coworkers want to hear from me? After all, I've only been coding for a couple of years."

"I only recently started using this framework."

"I'm new to my role."

"I'm not exactly well known outside of my company."

The list of reasons to back down goes on and on.

But people do want to hear about your unique experiences. They're curious about how you, with your personality and backstory, created a product, solved a problem, or took a critical step in your career. They want to learn and be inspired.

If people didn't want to learn from living, breathing speakers, performers, and teachers, they'd just stay at home and read a book. But many people go to talks because they're a new way to soak in information – and for some people, it's the most effective way to learn. Talks also expose attendees to new perspectives from people they wouldn't otherwise hear from, such as techies who don't have published books or blogs.

And then there's the beginner in the audience. There's always someone who is less experienced than you are, and they will want to learn from what you've done. Basically, they want to fast-track their own learning by hearing about your successes. They want to know how you acquired a skill they've been eyeing for themselves, what you wish you had known before you started a project, and what you would do differently if you had to do it all over again.

They also want to hear about what happens when things go wrong. While it can be hard for us to talk about our failures, big or small, audiences love hearing cautionary tales. They appreciate when you expose the reasons why something you tried didn't work out, and what you did to remedy a problem.

Ultimately, people want to hear presentations that are authentic and based on true experiences. And we know you have experiences to share.

## The best topic is what you already know

Here's our first time-saving tip: focus on what you already know.

Too often, people worry about coming up with topics that are new and novel, because they think that's what people want to hear. But when speakers try to cover something new to them, they end up adding a lot of time to the process of preparing their talk.

Why?

Simple: they need to go out and research the topic because they don't know anything about it.

Save yourself time by talking about what you already know. You come with experiences under your belt that are truly valuable to others. And the best topics are the ones that you are already enthusiastic about. Your pre-existing knowledge, combined with your natural interest, works wonders: you'll have fun preparing and giving your talk, and your audience will feel your enthusiasm and enjoy it.

 *I'm going to tell you about the worst talk I ever gave. When I think back on it, I get embarrassed all over again.*

*I was a manager at a software company at the time, and I needed to share the new company strategy with my team. I had seen my boss give a presentation on it, so I decided to give the same presentation at my next team meeting. I asked for his slides, scheduled the meeting, and marched in with my laptop and my notes. And I bombed. I didn't practice, I wasn't comfortable with this presentation that someone else had created, and I couldn't answer most of the questions.*

*I'll never give someone else's presentation again. In fact, the next year, when we had another company strategy to announce, I took an entirely different tack. I gathered stories of the business challenges our customers were facing and used them to explain the strategy. And this time, I didn't use any slides.*

*Afterward, someone asked me if I had taken a class in public speaking. I guess the difference was pretty noticeable.*

There are plenty of things to speak about:

- **Technical topics** such as programming languages and frameworks, design methodologies, and product-building tools

- **Tech business topics** such as customer needs and content marketing

- **Personal development topics** such as strategies to thrive in your career and find creative expression as a techie

## Find an experience to talk about with the Inventory Method

The **Inventory Method** is a way to reflect on your past experiences to find a talk topic. We like this approach because it helps find problems that others in your field are likely to experience as well.

Here's a simple example of how Poornima took stock of her recent work projects and created a talk based on an experience she had.

*Back in 2008, I wanted to get back into public speaking. But I had been pretty heads down building Mint.com, so I wasn't sure what to talk about.*

*After stepping back to examine the last few months of my life and talking to a few people about topics, I realized that I had a very unique experience: scaling a prototype into a product used by millions.*

*So I sat down and wrote out what I had learned while scaling Mint and some of the challenges I survived. I wrote about the technologies I used to build the prototype and how we eventually scaled the prototype from serving just a few folks to serving millions.*

*I also jotted down the type of person who I thought could benefit from this.*

*Then I formulated it into a talk and delivered it at Silicon Valley Code Camp in 2008.[6] People in the audience found it valuable because the majority had never worked at a startup or built a prototype that needed to scale fast. Many had only built a prototype or had worked on a product that had already been scaled to serve many people. So it was great to bridge the gap and share my experience with them.*

Give the Inventory Method a whirl with this activity.

# PRACTICE
## INVENTORY METHOD

Extract your expertise with the Inventory Method to find a topic for your talk.

Start by taking stock of your past projects from the last six to twelve months and list them (you can also include significant projects from another time if you have some in mind).

**Pick one project on your list and answer these questions**

1. **What was the purpose of the project?**
   What problems did your project aim to solve?
   What were your goals?

2. **What were your particular contributions?**
   If you were part of a team, what were your contributions to the project?

3. **What were your challenges?**
   What troubles did you face? Was there a challenge that got you or your team stuck? How did you jump over these hurdles? Did you adopt a new technology or create a new process?

# PRACTICE CONTINUED

4. **What did you learn, and how did you learn it?**
   How did you get started on a new technology, programming language, market segment, or career skill? Did you take a class? What books, websites, or other resources did you find helpful?

5. **What's your advice to others in your shoes?**
   What advice do you have for people doing a similar project? What do you wish you had known before you started? What would you do differently if you had to do it all over again? What are your cautionary tales?

Review your answers about this project. Is there enough here to create a talk? How long would it be?

If you struggled to come up with clear answers, pick a different project and go through the questions again. When you find a topic with enough material, that's your tentative talk idea.

## Take a stance

When you speak, you need to make clear and convincing points. If you're wishy-washy, people will leave your talk confused or even irritated that they wasted their time attending it. They prefer hearing strong opinions, so when you craft your talk, take a stance and stick to it.

*While I was a Venture Partner at 500 Startups, I noticed that several startup founders were struggling to build a pipeline of prospects. Their main problem was that they were going after the wrong types of customers: people who didn't have a budget, were happy with other products, or just didn't care enough to invest in a solution.*

*Telling someone that they are doing something wrong is demotivating to begin with, and if I had left them with nothing but a little lukewarm advice, they'd think I had wasted their time. These founders were doers looking for techniques they could trust.*

*To appeal to my audience of founders, I focused on the outcome they wanted to achieve: closing customers. I made it crystal clear by titling my talk "How to Build a Sales Pipeline with Customers You Can Close" (you can see the slides and audio in the ★ Present! interactive bundle).*

*To reinforce the title, I began the talk by telling the audience about three takeaways:*

*1. How to find prospective customers effectively*

*2. How to handle objections*

*3. How to push past revenue plateaus*

*For each takeaway, I took a strong stance to keep them engaged. Take my first point, for example. I know that people hate prospecting. It's time consuming and rife with rejection. So instead of trying to make it sound romantic, I took the stance that you don't have to like it – you just have to do it. Because if you don't do it, you won't get anywhere. But if you do it, get rejected, and learn from the rejections, you'll be better equipped the next time you have a conversation.*

*In the second takeaway, I pointed out that people often ignore a prospect's objections. They just go in for the kill without understanding why the objections exist. Instead of steamrolling over them, it's important to take the time to get to know the prospect's concerns and see whether you can address them.*

*Finally, people often think that the tactics that got them their first amount of revenue are the same ones that will get them the next, larger amount. I asserted that to make a serious jump in revenue, you have to attract a new base of customers and run new experiments. To bolster my point, I shared anecdotes of the companies I'd helped get to $1,000 in monthly recurring revenue, and then how I helped them get to $10,000 in monthly recurring revenue. Showing the tactical differences between the two phases strengthened my stance.*

*After the talk, people expressed gratitude that I presented a viewpoint that I believed in and backed it up with examples.*

## You don't have to be an expert

With all this talk about finding your "expertise," you might worry that you don't know everything about a particular topic.

Well, you're right. You don't know everything. Most experienced speakers don't either, and that's okay. Your goal is simply to take a complex problem that you've personally struggled with and help the audience understand it.

You want them to have an easier time with the problem if or when they encounter it themselves. They will get these benefits if you clearly break down a problem and possible solutions, whether or not you wrote the book on the field. Audiences love clarity, especially when you're working with abstract and technical concepts.

All you have to do is stay true to your qualifications and what you're certain you do know. Here are some ways to keep your topic within the scope of your knowledge and make sure that your audience has the right expectations for your talk.

- Narrow the scope of your talk to a subset of a topic and verbalize what you will and will not cover. This might feel like you're copping out of explaining a broader, tougher subject that you could cover if only you knew more, but remember that there will be people who want to learn about the specific sliver you know plenty about.

- When you're creating your proposal and promoting your talk, clarify who should be sitting in the audience. You can even do this when you start your talk. If it's for beginners, say so, and then advanced people will know that your talk may not be for them (and vice versa).

- Offer resources that people can check out for additional information on your topic.

If you've narrowed the scope of your talk, you might still get a question during a Q&A session that you're just not sure how to answer. We'll discuss how to handle this scenario and share other strategies to finesse Q&A in Chapter 12.

## It's okay if your talk topic isn't unique

You might be worried about giving a talk similar to one someone else has given recently, covering a topic that's often rehashed elsewhere, or having a subject that overlaps with another presentation at the same event you're speaking at.

Don't preemptively stop yourself from giving a talk for fear of having a redundant topic. Your unique background and perspective on a subject bring new value to your presentation, and people don't necessarily tire of hearing the same thing more than once, and from someone else.

In 2012, Poornima and one of her employees submitted a panel proposal to the SXSW conference in Austin, Texas. Their topic was about career generalists versus specialists: how some people change roles during their careers and develop a wide range of skills, while others are focused on specific areas and become experts.

Their proposal was accepted. But when they got to the conference, they noticed that there was another panel at the event on the exact same topic! They were worried that no one would show up to their talk and began to investigate why SXSW chose to host two redundant panels.

The conference organizers told them that it wasn't a big deal because the conference is so big. In fact, they do it on purpose. If conference attendees miss the first one, they can catch the second. Plus, the panelists planned for the other talk had different backgrounds.

If your proposal is accepted for a smaller conference and there's a similar topic, organizers will usually reach out to you and let you know. They'll often work with you to position your talk so that it's sufficiently different from the other presentation.

## Is your topic interesting?

Before settling on your topic and spending time on your proposal, you want some confidence that people will be interested in it. So here's another time-saving tip: don't start to write your talk or create a long proposal the moment you've come up with a good idea.

Instead, share a topic teaser with some people to judge their interest. We call this the Talk Topic Test. The topics for our talks often come from conversations we have. When we share a story or our experience with someone and they tell us they want to hear more, we know we have a possible presentation topic.

 *Earlier in my career, I told a colleague about a newfangled technology called an object-oriented database. To describe it, I compared this new style of database to a relational database. This explanation clicked for my colleague - his eyes lit up! And that was all the inspiration I needed to write a paper about my experiences with the two database technologies. I submitted my paper to an ACM conference; it was accepted, and I gave a talk about it on a very big stage. Sharing my topic idea and getting positive feedback gave me the motivation to go through with it.*

## Sample topic teasers for the Talk Topic Test

Here are sample teasers for talks we've given – we included titles, but they're not necessary yet.

> ### The Evolution of a Scrappy Startup to a Successful Web Service
>
> *"I'm thinking of giving a talk about how I built Mint.com's prototype and then scaled it to serve millions of users. It would be good for people who are product managers and engineers at startups that already have a basic product prototype working and want their product to support more people as they scale their user base. I'll share three key lessons I learned, a few fails to avoid, and which open source tools are best for this kind of project."*
>
> ### Learn to Build a Beautiful Prototype to Validate Your Product Idea
>
> *"I'd like to get your feedback on a talk I'm planning. It's about how startups often struggle to build an application end to end that they can showcase to potential customers to get validation. They worry about the time it takes to build a product demo: to get set up, learn a new framework, design it, and eventually deploy it. I'll walk startup founders through a quick step-by-step process for creating a prototype using the Ember.js framework and cover useful tools like Twitter Bootstrap for design."*

You'll notice that the first sample teaser mentions a personal story that illustrates the point. Sometimes, adding a personal story helps clarify the topic and pique people's interest, but if you don't have one, don't worry. It's not required for a simple topic test, and we'll help you add storytelling to your talk in Chapter 5.

In this activity, you'll create a teaser of your own. Don't worry too much about getting it perfect; we just want you to get your feet wet with an informal test.

# PRACTICE

## TALK TOPIC TEST

**Involves asking other people to give you feedback.**

The Talk Topic Test is a quick way to gauge whether your topic is interesting to your potential audience. Take the topic you found in the Inventory Method and create a teaser with this formula. Then bring it up in conversation with one or two friends or coworkers and check whether it resonates with them.

1. **Create a topic teaser**
   Grab a pen or keyboard and jot down three to four sentences about your topic that hit the following points:

   - **Describe the problem**
     In one or two sentences, explain the project worked on and the challenge you faced.

   - **Who is it for?**
     Who would benefit from hearing this talk?
     Who is your target audience?

   - **What will you cover?**
     What are you going to share during your talk? Do you have any advice or takeaways you want your audience to walk away with? Keep this to one or two sentences as well.

# PRACTICE CONTINUED

2. **Share it**

   Tie it all together in your mind and share it with one or two coworkers or friends who are representative of the audience you have in mind, or at least are in your general field. It's best if you tell someone about the proposed talk or read it out loud rather than sending the paragraph in an email.

3. **Observe the reaction**

   Watch their body language and facial expressions to see how interested they are and what parts might confuse them.

4. **Ask for feedback**

   Find out what parts they liked and what you can do to improve the topic. Or, determine whether you should toss it and find a different one (then repeat this exercise).

A quick note before you move on: make sure you have permission to speak about a topic if it's related to your company. Do you need to get approval before talking about it? Did you sign a non-disclosure agreement that limits what you can say about a project? If you're not sure, seek advice from your manager or a legal expert.

# RECAP

## CHAPTER 3

### Audiences want to hear about your real-life experiences

1. Look for a topic where you can discuss a problem you've already grappled with. Break it down clearly and lay out your solutions (and failures). If your audience is struggling with the same issue or could encounter it in the future, your experience will help them.

2. Use the **Inventory Method** to find experiences and expertise you can share.

### Save time by validating your talk before you develop it fully

- Use the **Talk Topic Test** to create a short teaser of your topic and share it with people to gauge whether it interests them.

# 4

# IDENTIFY YOUR IDEAL AUDIENCE

Once you have a topic and are confident that it's interesting, figure out who your ideal audience is and guarantee that your talk will provide them with awesome value.

It's crucial that you have a target audience in mind as you formulate your proposal in the next chapter. Without it, you will struggle to put crisp takeaways and calls-to-action into your talk. Or, you might miss the mark altogether and give a fantastic presentation that doesn't resonate with the people in the room.

The goal here is to help you figure out who will care about your talk, pinpoint exactly how you can help them, and then build on your topic teaser from Chapter 3 to attract your target audience and appeal to event organizers who cater to the same population.

## Why is audience focus important?

Picking a target audience and crafting a presentation for them lets you attract the right people to your talk and make sure they leave satisfied.

Audience focus makes it easier to write a compelling proposal for your talk and open doors to cool speaking opportunities. Conference organizers want to know that you've thought about the

---

needs of the audience and the takeaways. You'll make it easy for them to accept you.

People will praise you for how thoroughly you've thought through their needs. They'll see that you understand their problems and took the time to come up with solutions. It shows that you care about them and their success when you go above and beyond by anticipating their questions and collecting helpful resources and stories beforehand.

You'll appear as if you are thinking on your feet during Q&A. Many of our students are concerned about their ability to nimbly answer questions while they're onstage. When you anticipate audience needs, prepare answers to common queries, and have helpful resources on hand, you'll be able to field most questions with ease.

You'll be known as a specialist. Serving a specific audience, a niche, makes you the go-to expert for that group of people.

Last year Poornima was asked to present on a rather big topic at the Women 2.0 HowTo Conference. In the story below, she explains how she narrowed the focus of her talk, how it resonated with the audience, and how she appeared to be thinking on her feet during the Q&A period.

 *Last year I was invited to present at the Women 2.0 HowTo Conference. They gave me thirty minutes to explain how companies go from a product idea to product launch. That's a big topic because there are so many steps and a lot of different roles that contribute to it. To keep the talk focused, I decided to speak directly to startup founders.*

*I planned to give them how-to takeaways in three key areas:*

- *Attract technical talent*
- *Attract paying customers*
- *Fund product development*

*I shopped my talk idea around to aspiring and existing startup founders and asked them what questions were top of mind for them. They asked things like, "Can I get someone to work for sweat equity?" "Where can I find technical talent?" "Can I get customers to pre-pay for my product?" "When is a good time to seek VC funding?" and so on.*

*I found the answers to the questions and then tried to address many of them in the talk itself. But I couldn't answer them all because it would expand the talk too much. I figured I could address them during the Q&A if they came up, and sure enough, plenty of them did. Since I had prepared answers, I appeared to be thinking on my feet, and the audience really valued the fact that I could resolve their questions quickly.*

*After the talk, many people came up to me and asked to learn more. I directed them to my course and my book, and I gave them my contact information to follow up with me. It was a great step toward becoming a go-to resource for this subset of startup founders.*

## Clarify who your target audience is

These five considerations help you focus on the right audience:

1. **Audience persona**

   If you've ever built a product or done a marketing campaign, then you're probably familiar with "user personas," or profiles of your target customers. Here, you want to develop what we call an "audience persona," a short description of your ideal audience member.

   You'll want to describe straightforward attributes like their age, gender, and profession, as well as deeper characteristics like their goals, skills, attitudes, culture, and the environments (work or otherwise) in which they would apply what they learn in your talk.

2. **Audience motivation**

   Someone's motivation for attending your talk boils down to the problems in their life and the solutions your talk explores. Why are they here, and what's their interest in your topic or the problem you're discussing? What are the exact reasons that your talk would be important to them?

3. **Audience experience level**

   Decide how advanced your talk is and then lay out who the talk is and is not for, as well as any prerequisites (specific experiences that you require). If you're giving an advanced talk, you don't want beginners to show up and look confused. If you're giving a beginner talk, you don't want advanced audience members to walk out from boredom.

4. **Audience takeaways**

   Decide on one to three takeaways from your talk. These should relate back to the audience's motivation and act as solutions to their problems. Keep the list short and focused.

If appropriate, you can include a blend of basic and advanced takeaways, even if your audience's experience level is "beginner" – this appeals to both those who want to stay at the beginner level and those who want to go the extra mile.

5. **Audience questions**
Anticipate common questions people might have about a topic. These can be based on your own questions that you asked when you started working on the project that forms the subject of your talk, or you can ask people what questions they have about the topic (e.g., when you do the Talk Topic Test from Chapter 3).

It can also be helpful here to address solutions that you've tried without success, which can save people hours of frustration. For those questions that you don't cover in the talk, collect resources where you can point your audience for more help.

To illustrate, Karen recently used these five elements to flesh out a career development talk on embracing professional risk titled "Turn Risks into Opportunities":

*Audience persona: My target audience was female engineers and product managers working in the tech industry who wanted to take more risks in their careers but didn't know how.*

*Audience motivation: I set the context with an explanation of why women tend to avoid risk while pointing out that it can be risky not to take risks and keep doing what you've always done. I drew an analogy to what happened to Blockbuster back when Netflix disrupted the video rental industry.*

*Audience experience level: As I did my Talk Topic Test pre-work, I realized that women at all stages of their careers were finding my topic interesting, so I set my level broadly: women working in the tech industry at any stage of their career.*

*Audience takeaways: I collected stories from a handful of technical women who had taken big risks and what they had done to evaluate or mitigate the risks. I then extracted the approaches that each of these women took, boiled them down into discrete lessons, and turned them into my takeaways.*

*Audience questions: Again, the pre-work helped me here. As I talked to people about my topic and conversationally shared the stories I had collected, I took note of the questions people asked as they imagined applying the same strategies to their lives. I planned to address those questions in my talk.*

## Your audience influences your talk style

As you can see, thinking through who your audience is and what they need to learn can greatly impact the content of your talk. It can also influence your delivery style.

When we speak to professionals at a conference or give a talk at a company, we know our audience is filled with busy people who value their time. So we keep our presentations professional and to the point. We tell stories, but they are short. We often use slides (though not always) and provide an agenda about what we'll cover during the talk. And we take the time to showcase our backgrounds to establish credibility.

Contrast that to when we're speaking in front of college students. We're casual, because the last thing they want to listen to is another person with a slide deck telling them what to do. So we stand in front of them, without slides, and speak for twenty to thirty minutes. They're attentive and engaged, they ask smart questions, and they learn something.

*The first talk I ever gave at my alma mater, Duke University, was five years after I had graduated. I was on campus recruiting for my startup Mint.com, and I figured the best way to differentiate my startup from the sea of companies who were recruiting at the time was to give a talk at the engineering school. I contacted the department and asked if I could come in to give a talk, and they were thrilled that I had reached out and volunteered to present.*

*I recalled that I had always been bored by alumni who would just walk the audience through slide decks. They never really showed off their personalities, so by the end of the talk, we would be eager to jump out of our seats and leave rather than stay and ask questions during the Q&A or get to know the speaker.*

*I wanted to connect with the students who would be in my audience, so I decided to try a different format. I prepared a twenty-minute talk for the students with no slides. It was called "From Duke to Mint: The Blue She-Devil and Successful Startup."[7]*

*I kept it short because I wanted to give the audience ample time for Q&A. I hoped that if my talk had engaged them, they'd want to ask questions. And I chose not to present any slides so that they would watch me instead, picking up on my body language and movements.*

*I also thought this format would be more inspiring, and they could imagine themselves in five years being at the front of the room speaking to students about what they had accomplished in that span of time.*

*Turns out I had chosen the right approach. During Q&A, hands shot up pretty quickly, and after the talk, a number of students came up to me. They said that they were happy to come out and just see me speak instead of giving a long-winded presentation with slides.*

*One student in particular, Joe, wrote to me afterward and said, "Great presentation today to MEMP [Duke's Master's in Engineering Management Program]. It really showed that you had rehearsed it well. I would have expected the same delivery and poise from a CEO twice your age, but not from an engineer. You also gave me and other entrepreneurial MEMP students inspiration to keep working on our own IT ventures with the balance of our waking hours, so many thanks."*

*From that experience, I learned how impactful it can be to think like my audience and present in a style and format that appeals to them.*

Imagine yourself in a seat watching your talk. Think about how you can tweak elements of your style to fit your audience. Consider whether you'll use slides, whether you'll incorporate humor, how instructional you'll be, whether you'll include audience participation, and how you'll use your body and voice (more on this in Chapter 10).

# PRACTICE

## FOCUS YOUR TALK TOPIC FOR THE AUDIENCE

Grab a pen and paper or computer to create a profile of your ideal audience member. You can make it as long as you need to.

1. **Audience persona**

   Write out a short description of a typical audience member. Consider their profession, age, gender, culture, goals, skills, attitudes, and environments (work or otherwise).

2. **Audience motivation**

   What are some problems your ideal audience member might encounter? Do you have solutions or tips for them? List the reasons why they should listen to your talk.

3. **Audience experience level**

   Will your material be for beginners, experts, or somewhere in between? If needed, mention specific and clear prerequisites for your talk. For example, if you are giving a talk on Android development and want to make sure everyone has some knowledge of the framework, you could clarify the ideal level with something like, "Must be comfortable creating a simple Hello World application in Android."

# PRACTICE CONTINUED

4. **Audience takeaways**
   What will your audience learn from your talk?
   Are there any shortcuts they should try or avoid?
   Will you leave them with any how-tos?

   List takeaways and make them as concrete as possible.

5. **Audience questions**
   Anticipate the audience's needs. What are the most common questions you can think of? Do you have any helpful outside resources to share? What do you wish you had known before you worked on this project?

Next, reread your topic teaser from the Talk Topic Test. Compare it to the specific insights you wrote down in this activity. If needed, revise your topic to reflect your target audience and their needs.

# RECAP

## CHAPTER 4

**Talks are always better if they serve a specific audience**

Identify your ideal audience and focus on their needs. Narrowing focus helps you attract the type of people who will get the most out of your talk.

**Paint a portrait of your target audience member with five aspects:**

1. Audience persona

2. Audience motivation

3. Audience experience level

4. Audience takeaways

5. Audience questions

# 5

# TELL A STORY

Storytelling is one of the best strategies for engaging an audience, helping them remember your lessons, and making lessons easy to implement.

In this chapter, you'll learn the basic elements of a good story, find at least one to accompany your talk, and use it to crystallize the key messages you want to convey. It will ideally be a personal story you've experienced, although a well-told story about another person or group can be equally powerful.

## Stories supercharge your lessons

Stories are powerful for many reasons.

- They help the audience empathize with a problem

  When listeners hear about a problem, they'll play with it, try to solve it in their minds, and become engaged with what you're saying. If you just say you're a security expert who solved a DDoS problem, then there is nothing for them to do. You keep them passive. But if you start with "We were under attack - it was a DDoS," they're thinking, "Oh my gosh, there's a problem here ... how would I solve it, how did they solve it?"

- **They are relatable**
  When you share a story, it humanizes a technical problem. Remember, people are coming out to hear you. If you just lay out a bunch of facts and solutions, they will tune out. They can find this information online or in a book. They're coming out to hear you speak because they want to hear about your unique experience. So share that with them. Tell them what it was like to experience an issue, the challenges you grappled with while trying to solve it, and how you ultimately resolved it.

- **They make abstract ideas concrete**
  Whether you're presenting technical or business information, it's really easy for things to stay abstract and for the audience to leave without sufficient instruction to apply their newfound knowledge. But when you share a story of how you applied the abstract idea to a particular situation, the listeners now have an example that is clear in their minds.

- **They are memorable and repeatable**
  When you captivate an audience with your story, they remember it and share it with others. "I just saw so-and-so's talk. They talked about how they sidestepped a whopper of a security breach just six months ago." The person listening to them will ask, "Oh, what kind of security breach?" You reach more people when you give your audience a little something to talk about.

## Pick stories that evoke emotions

If you can make your audience feel an emotion, your points will be more relevant and memorable. Don't be afraid to share personal stories, proud moments, or infuriating situations. Show the audience that you're human.

---

To enhance the emotional side of a story, try the body and voice techniques in Chapter 10. For example, you can use strategic pauses during suspenseful points in your presentation, allow your voice to change between serious and lighthearted, and use gestures that mirror what you're saying to underscore your point.

## A note on humor

Funny stories help you connect with your audience, but tread carefully: humor can go wrong and turn the audience off.

Humor has to be natural. Don't force it; it might take some work to find something funny to say and some time to get comfortable enough to sprinkle it in.

It can also be taken the wrong way. You never know who will take offense to a joke, so here's a tip on keeping it safe: make fun of yourself, not someone else. This is why you'll hear us talk about spilling salsa on our shirts right before a talk!

To get more help with presenting humor in a natural way and finding good things to joke about, check out Jerry Seinfeld's documentary *Comedian*.[8] You'll learn how popular comedians prepare, find material, and perform.

*If you can get the audience to laugh, I recommend not laughing along with them. It can be bit unsettling to the crowd. Believe me, I made this mistake during my TEDx talk.*

*At one point, I misspoke, saying that, due to unconscious bias we believe "young boys are going to like girls" when I meant to say "young boys are going to like computers more than young girls are going to like them." I quickly corrected my mistake, and the audience and I laughed together.*

*Only, on the recording, my laugh is this loud guffaw and you can't even hear the audience. My advice? If you get your audience to laugh, shrug your shoulders and give a knowing smile, just like Amy Poehler and Tina Fey at the 2015 Golden Globes.[9]*

## Consider kicking off your talk with an anecdote

Hook your listeners from the very beginning with a story. Too often, people begin their talks by saying something like, "Hi, I'm so-and-so, and I'm a security expert." Then they dive right into technical topics.

While it's important to establish credibility and eventually share all the technical details you came to present, this formal presentation structure makes the audience feel like they're being lectured. When we're being lectured, we start to doze off like college freshmen in a 300-person class.

Instead of diving into your lesson, start with some action: "Six months ago, we were under attack! My company was facing a DDoS – a distributed denial of service, which is a serious network attack that makes a server or network resource unavailable to users. It was our first one ever, and we weren't sure what to do."

Rather than talking about how you're a security expert, which the audience might find boring, capture their attention with an exciting event you personally experienced.

## How to structure your story

Start with a common problem. Your anecdote's basic issue needs to relate back to the ideal audience member we discussed in Chapter 4. Ask yourself, "Would my ideal audience member ever experience this situation?" Beware of sharing a story that is off-topic or so unique that it's unrelatable. Instead, imagine what people in roles similar to yours are struggling with, or think about teams who are working on a product that has a customer focus or business model similar to yours.

Examples of relatable problems include finding effective customer acquisition techniques, onboarding new employees, learning new programming languages and frameworks, and securing applications.

Next, create a **story arc**. This helps you find the key messages, the necessary details to include, and the best order to present them in. Structure it like this:

- Context
- Challenge
- Available solutions
- Final takeaways

### 1. Context

To set the context, explain the situation and the basic problem. In the earlier example, we talked about a security breach that happened six months ago inside an organization:

> *"Six months ago, we were under attack! My company was facing a DDoS, a serious network attack."*

## 2. Challenge

Then you want to introduce a challenge. In the example, the real challenge is that the security breach in question was the organization's first:

> *"It was our first, and we weren't sure what to do."*

We could add additional details about the challenge, such as:

> *"We didn't have a security expert on staff."*
>
> *"This was the most pernicious attack in history."*

## 3. Available solutions

Next, explain the available solutions to the problem. Describe how you evaluated your options and reveal how things played out.

> *"The experts will tell you to overprovision your bandwidth so that you can accommodate the surge in traffic that comes with a DDoS attack. Unfortunately, we hadn't done that. They'll also tell you to set up an early warning system for attacks, because the earlier you know about it, the easier it is to mitigate it. Right, except we hadn't done that either. We ended up calling our hosting provider in a panic."*

## 4. Final takeaways

Finally, close with what you learned from the experience, weaving in advice or words of wisdom.

*"After spending two all-nighters in a chat session with our hosting provider, I vowed to never go through that again. We now have an early warning system for DDoS attacks, a small team of trained DDoS leaders, and the budget to purchase twice our expected bandwidth needs every quarter."*

## The sinking ship of storytelling

Have you listened to someone tell a story and started to wonder, "Where is all this going?" They took a long time to set up the context, they took forever to introduce the problem at hand, and they went on tangents. You eventually tuned out.

Don't take too long to tell your story when you present. Otherwise, you're taking your audience for a ride on "the sinking ship of storytelling." You take so long to tell a story that your passengers decide to fling themselves overboard because they don't want to go down with a sinking ship.

To avoid this, you want to make sure that you're moving the story's main character, you or someone else, at a reasonable pace, never spending too much time in one state of the story arc before floating to the next. This progress builds exciting momentum for your talk.

There's no golden rule when it comes to how much time you should spend within each state, but at a high level, you can calculate how much time it takes to deliver the whole story. For example, if you're doing a five-minute lightning talk, then you wouldn't want to spend more than thirty to sixty seconds sharing a story. For longer talks, you need to make sure you can cover all your points along with the story. You'll know if you have to whittle things down once you start practicing (more on this in Chapter 8).

## Should you give it up all at once?

Starting your talk with a story is a great hook to get your audience listening. You can finish it at the beginning of the talk and move on to your teaching and lessons, never to reference your anecdote again. And this is okay. But if you want to be a presentation pro, make your presentation richer, and keep people at the edge of their seats, then refer back to your story periodically during your presentation.

We call this the Slow Reveal Technique. Instead of sharing all the states of the story up front, share one state at a time, along with a corresponding piece of your presentation's teaching content. You're essentially layering your story over your presentation piece by piece. Each major stage in your anecdote comes with a teaching point, and the anecdote ties all the lessons together and drives them forward.

 *After I wrote my first book, How to Transform Your Ideas into Software Products, several conferences asked me to present on how to go from product idea to prototype. I developed a talk and continue to deliver it around the world.*

*In the book, I present steps and accompany them with exercises, which makes the book easy to follow. But the steps are more boring when you're sitting in a forty-five-minute presentation. So instead of just presenting the steps, I walk the audience through a chronology of events based on how I developed the product for my second startup, BizeeBee, a CRM (customer relationship management) solution for fitness businesses like yoga studios.*

*I never present the entire story of how I went from idea to launch. Instead, I unveil parts of the story as I move from step to step. It grounds abstract ideas and keeps the audience engaged with each step. They are eager to hear what happened next.*

*For example, I start by talking about the process of ideation and why you need to have domain expertise. Then I tie in a short piece of the BizeeBee story: how I had been practicing yoga for a long time, volunteered at studios, and noticed some challenges studio owners face day in and day out. This gave me domain expertise.*

*Next, I talk about the importance of user interface testing. Since it's a challenge to recruit customers, I give the example of how I reached out to studio owners who were friends of mine and asked them to sit with me and review paper prototypes.*

*Finally, I describe how, when I had to monetize my product, I asked owners a series of questions to understand their reactions to possible price points.*

*Weaving in pieces of my experience at BizeeBee, going from idea to launching a prototype, gives the audience clear examples that they can carry with them and takes the guesswork out of how to make it happen on their own.*

To see great storytelling in action, we recommend you watch a TED talk called *"The Clues to a Great Story"*[10] by Andrew Stanton, the writer behind all the *Toy Story* movies, *Finding Nemo*, and *WALL-E*. When you watch it, you'll notice how Andrew layers his personal story into the presentation rather than delivering it all up front.

Ready to find your story? Use this activity to brainstorm anecdotes and work one into your talk.

# PRACTICE

## WHAT'S YOUR STORY?

Complete these steps to prepare a story for your talk. You can repeat them as many times as you need to if you have multiple stories in your talk.

### Pick your story

First, brainstorm stories and choose one.

1. Take out a pen and paper or your computer.

2. Brainstorm stories you can use to illustrate the problems and solutions in your talk. They don't need to be personal, but personal ones are often best.

3. Select a story. If there was one project at work or a personal experience that inspired the topic for your talk, try going with that one.

# PRACTICE CONTINUED

## Structure it

Unpack your story to find the points of suspense and valuable lessons. Jot down notes:

1. **Find the common problem**
   What's the problem in your story? Find a problem "category" that your audience will be able to relate to (e.g., finding customer acquisition techniques, onboarding new employees, learning new programming languages and frameworks, and securing applications).

2. **Create your story arc**
   - **Context**
     Set the scene with the basic issue at hand.
   - **Challenge**
     Highlight the challenge or hurdles you faced.
   - **Solutions**
     Go over the options available to you and explain how you arrived at a final solution.
   - **Final takeaways**
     Share lessons you learned, both from successes and failures.

# PRACTICE CONTINUED

## Record yourself telling your story

This helps you check whether you sound natural and are conveying the right details.

- Record yourself on your phone or computer.

- Talk through your story arc, keeping the story's length at two to four minutes (unless your talk has a specific time goal).

- Watch your recording. Did you meet time constraints? Did you tell the right details? Repeat recording yourself as necessary.

# RECAP

## CHAPTER 5

**Storytelling is a powerful complement to your talk's key messages**

Stories are relatable and memorable, make abstract ideas concrete, and keep the audience engaged. Your talk should have at least one.

**Use a story arc to organize an anecdote:**

1. Context

2. Challenge

3. Available solutions

4. Final takeaways

You can tell a story all at once, or use the **Slow Reveal Technique** to share pieces bit by bit throughout your presentation.

# 6

# PITCH YOUR TALK

The goal of submitting a speaking proposal is to convince a conference or event organizer to invite you to be a speaker. Persuasive proposals unlock access to more and more high-quality speaking opportunities so you can establish your expertise faster and make better connections.

So now that you have a topic, key takeaways, and at least one story, weave them together into a formal proposal that packs a punch.

We recommend that you develop your proposal at this stage in the process – after nailing down your topic but before fleshing out the talk itself – for two reasons.

First, you can recycle parts of it to form the foundational outline of your presentation, helping you create a logical structure and flow (you'll do this in the next chapter). Second, it saves you time. When you submit a proposal, the reviewers may give you feedback on your suggested talk that sends you back to the drawing board or requires you to rework a section. If you create the talk before the proposal, you may have to throw away work, or worse, you may have developed a talk that won't be approved at all.

The first step is to find speaking opportunities. Then, we'll show you how to create a professional and tailored proposal.

## Find speaking opportunities

To find speaking opportunities, the first step is to let people know that you want to speak in public. Tell your coworkers and friends. Put it in your LinkedIn summary statement. Mention it when you meet new people. If you're on a first-name basis with your barista, tell them too!

Next, look for events that need speakers. Your company or department may have a weekly all-hands meeting or a regular tech talk opportunity, and you may simply need to reach out to your manager or the person running the event to let them know you'd like to speak.

And in the tech world, conferences and events happen almost daily. The larger conferences will put out calls for proposals (CFPs) where they describe the kinds of talks they're looking for, the information they need, and how and when to submit proposals. Smaller events can be more casual, and organizers might be open to receiving pitches for a talk via email.

You can set up Google alerts, too. First try the keywords "lightning talks" or "call for proposals." Initially, you'll get a lot of hits, and later you can decide how to refine the searches for the audiences you want to speak to (e.g., "lightning talks for iOS developers").

You can also subscribe to newsletters and join online community groups that aggregate and share calls for proposals, such as Technically Speaking[11] (sign up for their newsletter or follow them at @techspeakdigest[12]) and Technical Women Speak Too.[13] Follow @CallbackWomen[14] on Twitter. Lanyrd[15] is a searchable website that lists upcoming conferences, and WikiCFP[16] aggregates calls for papers in science and technology. Visit them and search for topics you're interested in speaking about.

In this process, you might come across an "unconference." An unconference is an unstructured conference without pre-set schedules, formal proposals, and sponsor fees. Attendees convene for the informal exchange of information. A "talk" can range from a well-rehearsed slide deck presentation to a product demo to a group discussion to whiteboarding a new concept.

If you want to speak at an unconference, you'll need to do a little preparation so that you can convince the attendees to listen to your talk. (This is usually done day-of, though sometimes topics are proposed beforehand on a wiki.) Ultimately, though, it saves time. At an unconference, you can practice, develop, and test a talk quickly before investing a lot of energy in polishing a proposal and reaching out to organizers. You can search for unconferences on Lanyrd and learn how to prepare by checking out resources from organizations like Unconference.net.[17]

## Reach out to the organizer

Once you find an event that interests you, reach out to the organizer to check whether speaking opportunities still stand. This also gets you on their radar and gives you a chance to ask important, clarifying questions that will increase the chance that your proposal will be accepted.

A quick note: Before you write an email to the event organizer, check whether they already have a website that lays out proposal submission guidelines and resources. You don't want to ask them for information that is already public. You can often find this on pages like "Speak," "Call for Proposals," "Request for Proposals," or "Call for Speakers."

You'll want to check whether they've provided a sample proposal, proposal structure requirements, a submission deadline, and a date when you can expect to hear back from them. If you can't find this information online, ask for it in an email once you know that they're accepting submissions. Also, double-check whether the conference has unique submission guidelines - for example, the Lean Startup Conference[18] will ask you to submit a short video of you speaking about the specific topic you'd like to present at the conference.

The earlier you can contact the organizer to ask about opportunities, the better - many conferences recruit six to nine months ahead of time, and some of the bigger ones recruit a year in advance - but it's okay to contact the organizers closer to the event. Some of their speakers might have backed out at the last minute, and you may be just what they need.

Some conferences prefer to hand-select their speakers through word-of-mouth referrals rather than sifting through proposals. If that's the case, then you'll want to reach out to them early or see if you have mutual connections who can refer you to the event organizers.

However, a simple email will do the trick in most cases. The purpose is to check whether they have speaker availability and introduce yourself. You can offer to schedule a phone call to discuss more or simply ask for proposal requirements so you can get started. If you have a couple of talks under your belt with assets such as videos and slides, then share them up front. This helps organizers see your speaking style, and often they will request these samples anyway.

# PRACTICE
## INQUIRE ABOUT A SPEAKING OPPORTUNITY

Reach out to the organizer of an event you want to speak at to inquire about speaking opportunities and share your talk topic.

If you've given recorded talks in the past, link to them in your email (templates below). If you haven't, this is your chance to create a sample.

Record a short teaser video to share that's one to three minutes long (keep it short). The goal is to show that you are capable of speaking clearly and conversationally. The subject can be simple; you can talk about your topic's takeaways, tell a story you found in Chapter 5, or deliver your talk's introduction if you already know how you want to structure it.

Once you're done, upload it to YouTube and link to the video in an email like this:

# PRACTICE CONTINUED

**Email template to reach out to an event organizer (with speaking sample video)**

Hi {name},

I noticed you're organizing {conference} in {nine} months. Are you still looking for speakers?

If so, I'd be interested in presenting about {topic}. I've created a short video to give you a sense of my speaking style: {link to video}.

If you'd like to have me speak, I'd be happy to jump on a call to discuss the opportunity further or review your proposal guidelines and deadlines over email.

Looking forward to hearing from you shortly!

Kindly,
{Your name}

# PRACTICE CONTINUED

**Email template to reach out to an event organizer (with links to your past talks)**

Hi {name},

I noticed you're organizing {conference} in {nine} months. Are you still looking for speakers?

If so, I'd be interested in presenting about {topic}. Here are a few talks I've given, along with sample videos and their slides.

Talk title 1, link to video, link to slides
Talk title 2, link to video, link to slides

If you'd like to have me speak, I'd be happy to jump on a call to discuss the opportunity further or review your proposal guidelines and deadlines over email.

Looking forward to hearing from you shortly!

Kindly,
{Your name}

## Create your proposal

Time to create your formal proposal. Here are the key elements (we'll explain them in detail below):

- Title
- Summary
- Takeaways
- Format and length
- Target audience
- Bio
- Headshot

Of course, a conference organizer may ask for some additional information based on their needs. If they provide you with a template, be sure to fill in everything they've requested.

### 1. Title
The best titles are catchy and pithy. You want your title to grab people's attention and make them interested in coming to your talk. This is especially important because many conference programs list nothing more than the title of a talk and the presenter's name, forgoing exciting descriptions or pictures.

Recently, Karen's friend was working on a proposal for a panel and asked for feedback. Her title was a mouthful – something like "Strategies and Methodologies for Surviving and Thriving in an Always-On, Global, 24x7 Workplace."

*Here's a pro tip:* Don't start your title with "Strategies and Methodologies." It's a bit formal and unnecessary.

*Another pro tip:* Make your title short.

Add some imagery if you can. Here's what Karen and her friend came up with as an alternative: "Lines in the Sand: Drawing Boundaries in a 24x7 Workplace." They found a great photo of lines in the sand to use on the presentation cover slide.

## 2. Summary

Your talk summary is an overview that includes the motivating factor behind your talk and why you're qualified to talk about it. It should be short, about three to five sentences. We often like to start our summaries with a question:

> *Need to scale your product prototype? I had to do this in record time for my first startup, Mint.com. In this talk, I'll share five strategies that can help you scale your app.*

## 3. Takeaways

Be clear about what people will get out of your talk. It's also a good time to mention additional resources you'll provide. For example:

> *In this talk, I will explain how to use the analytics dashboard and provide a handout of my favorite resources for those of you who want to integrate its API into your app.*

You can also present your talk takeaways as a list of three to five things the audience will learn (as paragraphs or bullets). For example, a technical talk about hosting a software product might teach the following:

> *I will explain:*
> - *How to evaluate hosting options*
> - *The tools I use to monitor the service*
> - *Two successful approaches to backing up data during a migration (and one that didn't work so well)*

Be clear about your takeaways, and don't expect the conference organizer to read your mind. The more understandable your takeaways are, the more likely it is that a conference organizer will accept your talk.

### 4. Format and length

Your proposal should state the format and length of your talk (and if you're applying to an event that specifies what type of talk they're looking for, reiterate it). These are some popular formats:

- **Lightning talk**
  A short, fast-paced talk that can be as short as two minutes or as long as seven minutes
- **Ignite talk**
  A specific format lasting five minutes with exactly twenty slides that advance automatically every fifteen seconds
- **Long-form talk**
  A more in-depth talk that lasts thirty to sixty minutes and tends to have plenty of time for Q&A
- **Keynote**
  A long-form talk where you are the main speaker for that part of the conference, conveying its main message and setting the tone
- **Panel**
  A collection of speakers on a topic with a moderator who asks questions and keeps the conversation moving along

## 5. Target audience

In one to two sentences, describe your ideal audience members and their level of experience with your topic.

Is your talk for beginners who have limited or no experience with Python? Is it for entrepreneurs who want to learn how to apply Lean Product Development techniques? Is it for product managers who want to deploy their successful US product in China? Don't expect the event organizers to predict whom your talk is for.

You don't want to confuse people who don't have the background you're expecting or bore people who have already learned the material you'll be teaching. Create a simple benchmark in your proposal (and you can repeat it again when you start speaking). For example, "This talk is for anyone who has written a Hello World application for Android."

 *I always make it a point to ask an event or conference organizer about their attendees before I get to work on my proposal so that I can tailor my submission and talk accordingly. A good organizer cares about having talks that fit the audience, so they are usually happy to oblige.*

*Here are a few key questions I ask:*

**How many people do you expect to be at the entire event, and how many might show up to my talk?**
*I want to know how big the event will be, and whether it's an intimate setting where I can be more casual, or on a stage in front of hundreds or thousands where my delivery needs to be a little more formal and rehearsed.*

**What are the backgrounds of the people attending?**
*Where do they work, and what do they do for a living?*

*This lets me think through what they might be experiencing and the day-to-day challenges they face.*

**What level are most people at for the subject I'm considering speaking about?**
*Beginner, intermediate, or advanced? As you know, it's important to craft the talk's complexity according to the audience's experience level.*

**Will the talk be live-streamed or recorded?**
*If other people will be watching the talk during or after the event, I need to make sure I can connect with them later via social media. I make sure to provide the audience with a Twitter hashtag, my contact information, and a link to the slides, if I have any.*

**Do you have samples of talks from previous years?**
*This lets me see the caliber of speakers and the types of talks they gave.*

*I also make it a point to check in with the organizer one or two weeks before the presentation to check whether anything has changed and modify my talk accordingly.*

## 6. Bio

Write a short professional bio that highlights your experience, and then add a special section that describes why you are qualified to speak about your topic for this event. Emphasize your credibility – the work you've done, positions you've held, articles you've published, and prior talks you've given. If you have videos of talks that you've given before, link to them in this section.

We have a cautionary tale to share about bios. Not too long ago, Karen proposed a panel on taking professional risks for the Grace Hopper Celebration. She assembled an amazing group of four women who each had stories about how they learned to take risks and had recommendations on how to deal with risk, and she created a great proposal. But it wasn't accepted.

The feedback from the reviewers said that while the topic was excellent, they didn't understand why the panelists would be qualified to speak on taking risk. Karen took full responsibility for this fail; she had asked each panelist to send her a bio of their professional accomplishments, but she didn't ask them to include something about the big risk they had taken and what they learned.

From that point on, she decided she would never make that mistake again. Now, she and her panelists always take time to create a custom bio that reflects the experiences that relate to the talk's specific subject.

## 7. Headshot

Last but not least, include a headshot. When we say headshot, we don't mean a selfie you took with your phone. The reason we recommend this is not for vanity. People need to see who the speaker is on their paper programs and online and be able to identify them once they enter the room. A clear headshot goes a long way, so take the time to get a professional one. If you work for a company, ask whether they offer headshot photo sessions for employees. Alternatively, get photo studio and photographer recommendations from friends who have great social media profile pictures.

Make sure the picture is high resolution, and if possible, have both color and grayscale versions, because often the print version of your picture will show up in black and white in conference programs.

## Sample proposals

Here are two sample proposals. Below, you'll find an activity to guide you through writing your own.

**Title**
*Be More Strategic! Stories & Tips from Experienced Technical Women*

**Summary**
*Have you been told you need to be more "strategic"? If so, welcome to the club! Regardless of your role, your career can suffer if you don't take strategic steps to progress it. You might not be included in meetings, considered for projects, or invited to customer visits, and you might miss out on promotions.*

*Come hear from women who doubted their strategic ability at some point in their careers and hear how they overcame this to move in the right direction.*

**Takeaways**
*Our goal is for the audience to leave inspired and empowered to become stronger strategic thinkers. They will learn what being strategic means in their professional roles, how they can learn to think strategically, and how to drive their careers forward.*

**Format and length**
*This presentation will be a panel of four guests and one moderator. The total length will be fifty-five minutes, including fifteen minutes of Q&A.*

**Audience**

*This career panel is for employees who want to be more strategic in any role and at any experience level.*

**Bio: Panel moderator**

*Karen Catlin is an advocate for women in the tech industry. She's a leadership coach and a gender diversity advisor. Formerly, Karen was a VP at Adobe in the CTO's office, and she was CEO of Athentica, an early-stage online learning startup. She's learned through personal experience how to be strategic in her career, both in big-company and startup settings.*

*Karen is a TEDx speaker and a frequent presenter at women's leadership conferences. She has published articles in Fast Company, Inc., The Daily Beast, Women 2.0, and Femgineer. In 2015, she received the Wonder Women Tech Innovator Award from the California State Assembly for outstanding achievements in business and technology, and for being a role model for women.*

*Karen holds a degree in Computer Science from Brown University.*

*Headshot*

*Figure 6.1*

## Title
*Taking the Time to Tinker*

## Summary

*Many great innovations began as toys built by individuals who love to tinker. My own introduction to technology began when I was a child. At home, I wasn't afraid to take things apart; I even programmed the VCR and installed the sound card in my family's first PC.*

*While many people use technology, they fear learning how to code and build things. Machines are seen as a black box that should be left alone!*

*We need to reignite people's curiosity and imagination by getting back to engineering's roots – tinkering and playing with things to see how they work.*

## Takeaways
*The audience will learn:*

- *How tinkering can benefit ourselves and society*

- *Why we are afraid to tinker as a child, and why it only gets worse as we get older*

- *How we can overcome our fear and keep it at bay from childhood to adolescence and then into adulthood*

## Audience
*This is for anyone interested in playing with any kind of technology. The talk is suitable for all levels, from*

beginners to people who have advanced experience with technology and want to be more innovative.

## Format and length
*Fifteen-minute talk with no Q&A.*

## Bio
*Poornima has been fascinated by technology since she was three. Her father was a hardware engineer who made "chips" and "wafers," which she thought were potato chips and cookies. He took her to the fabrication facility when she was nine, where she watched how chips and wafers were tested. She was utterly amazed by the machines (and not too disappointed by the lack of treats). Inspired by what technology could do for humanity, she double-majored in Electrical Engineering and Computer Science at Duke University. She then moved to Silicon Valley, where she was lured into startup land. She was the founding engineer at Mint.com, and since its acquisition, she has started BizeeBee, a CRM solution for fitness businesses, and Femgineer, an education company for tech professionals and entrepreneurs.*

## Headshot

*Figure 6.2*

Now it's your turn to create a proposal for your talk. Make sure to complete this activity before continuing, even if you don't have an event you'd like to speak at. It will clarify the most important points of your talk and make it easier to write a talk outline in the next chapter.

# PRACTICE

## CREATE A PROPOSAL

Create a practice proposal

1. **Title**

   Describe your talk topic clearly and succinctly. Make it catchy.

2. **Summary**

   Write three to five sentences that reveal the motivation behind your talk and why you are qualified to speak.

3. **Takeaways**

   List takeaways that preview what the audience will learn.

4. **Format and length**

   State your talk's type, length, and Q&A time (if applicable).

5. **Audience**

   Describe your audience and what level of expertise they should have with the topic.

6. **Bio**

   Include a bio that shows off your topic-related qualifications.

7. **Headshot**

   Get a professional headshot that clearly shows your face.

# RECAP

## CHAPTER 6

### Create a proposal before developing your talk

If you write a proposal before you write the talk itself, you'll clarify the presentation structure (and potentially save time by getting an event organizer to give your topic the green light in advance).

Typical proposals include these elements:

1. Title
2. Summary
3. Takeaways
4. Format and length
5. Target audience
6. Bio
7. Headshot

# 7
# DEVELOP YOUR TALK

By now, you know exactly why people will want to (or better, need to) attend your talk. You have helpful takeaways, a story to illustrate them, and a proposal to convince an event organizer that their audience will benefit from hearing you speak.

It's time to outline your talk content and figure out what to say minute to minute.

## Focus on content before polish

In this chapter, you'll create an outline of your talk and your stories. This goes hand in hand with the following chapter, where you'll speak your outline out loud for the first time and edit the content as you practice it.

Focus on your content before you add polish; it saves time. As you practice, you'll cut pieces and move sections around, so it's not helpful to fuss over your physical and verbal delivery until your main points and stories are stage-worthy and you've practiced them.

So, make sure to complete Chapters 7 and 8 together to fully develop your talk content before moving on to Part III, where you'll learn how to enhance your presentation with gestures, walking, vocal inflections, and more.

Same goes for slides, which are meant to accent your presentation (we provide guidance on creating slides in Chapter 11). Slides can become a crutch if you create them before or in tandem with the actual content of your talk. If for some reason there is a technical glitch and you can't use your deck, you'll feel thrown off. So get used to practicing your presentation without slides. This will also save you time when creating slides because you'll know the best order and content to include.

Ready to get started? Let's structure your talk with an outline.

## Outlines, not scripts

We teach our students to develop their talk content in an outline format and to never turn it into a written script for memorization. Practicing from an outline can seem scary because it doesn't hold your hand the way a script does. But it leads to better delivery – one that's smooth, conversational, and adaptable if things go wrong.

If you write a script, you'll end up memorizing every word of your talk, which isn't ideal. Here's why.

- Rote memorization is risky because if you forget one line or even just one word, it can throw you off completely.

- There may be times where you have to alter your talk on the fly to fit the audience's needs. Memorization can hinder improvisation.

- Most people who memorize don't sound conversational or natural when they're speaking because they're using all their mental energy to remember the next line of their talk. When you think about how you speak in everyday conversation, you're not replaying a script in your head. You're simply thinking and speaking, and that's our goal.

- You'll have a harder time being present, observing the audience's reactions, and enjoying your experience.

There's one important exception: We do recommend that you memorize the first ten to fifteen seconds of your talk because the beginning is always the hardest on people's nerves. Aim to know your introduction cold so that you can launch into your talk with confidence and keep your nerves at bay.

## Outline structure

Your entire talk's outline structure will have the following sections:

- Introduction
  This is your talk's opening. For example, you can lead with a story or welcome the audience.

- Motivation
  Preview the takeaways to show the audience the benefits they will get if they sit up and pay attention.

- Takeaways
  Create a section for each takeaway. They will form the "meat" of your talk, and stories will go into these sections.

- Conclusion
  Recap the takeaways to help the audience remember them, make any final statements, raise forward-looking questions, and give the audience a call-to-action. What do you want them to do when they leave the talk?

Each section in the outline gets a subheading so it's easy to read.

Review your proposal; the same takeaways that you listed there become their own subheadings.

Within each one, you'll list supporting bullets or short phrases that you plan to hit, much like you would if you were starting to write a report or paper. Your outline will go from more detailed to less detailed as you refine it and practice it. So, your first draft can include quotes you want to use, stats, or any particular information you want to remember to talk about. However, it should not be a script. If your outline is made of paragraphs, then you're headed in the wrong direction.

At the end of the chapter, we'll provide an activity to guide you through the outline creation process.

## Sample outline

Here is a sample outline from Poornima's TEDx talk, "Taking the Time to Tinker."[19] This was the talk's first outline, so she included lots of details, including explanations of stories (she used three) and full quotes. As she practiced the talk, she became less reliant on notes and eventually weaned herself off the outline altogether.

> **Introduction**
>
> **Story #1**
> *A personal anecdote to showcase my own journey of how I started tinkering as a child between the ages of three and ten (spend three minutes on this story)*
>
> **Transition**
> *Talk about how it inspired me to pursue engineering and creating products like Mint.com, BizeeBee, and now Femgineer*

## Motivation

*No matter what our ages and backgrounds, we should all take time out of our busy schedules to tinker*

- *Tinkering doesn't have to be a formal process*
  - *It can be playful*
  - *You can start small and simple*
  - *The goal is to be curious and discover something new over time*
- *When we consistently take the time to tinker and build up knowledge, it can lead us down a path of new discoveries*
- *May turn into products that benefit us and society*

## Takeaways

- *Remember that tinkering can benefit ourselves and society*
- *The fear of tinkering starts in childhood, and it only gets worse as we get older (explain why)*
- *How to overcome fear of tinkering and keep it at bay from childhood to adolescence and then into adulthood*

## Takeaway #1

*"You don't need to have a formal education or a professional background to tinker."*

## Story #2

*Highlight how the Wright brothers, Orville and Wilbur, didn't have a formal education or a professional background*

- *Curious children; family encouraged intellectual development.*

- *"We were lucky enough to grow up in an environment where there was always much encouragement to children to pursue intellectual interests; to investigate whatever aroused curiosity." - Orville Wright (source: Orville's memoir)*
- *Father brought home a toy helicopter, which inspired them.*
- *Orville was fascinated by kites and began making his own at home.*
- *Studied work of famous German aviator Otto Lilienthal; Lilienthal died in a glider crash*
- *Brothers thought that improving aviation design would make flight possible*
- *Moved to Kitty Hawk, North Carolina.*
  - *Tinkered with wings*
  - *Observed birds*
  - *Wing warping*
  - *Moveable rudder*
  - *Developed new design*
  - *First in flight*

## Lesson

*Tinkerers change the world and impact human lives! And they don't need to be of a certain educational or professional background.*

## Takeaway #2

*Why we might be afraid to tinker as children*

### What stops kids from tinkering:

- *We are told not to touch this or that*
- *Ridiculed by other kids*

- *Considered aimless or antisocial by adults who aren't aware of opportunities and their need to explore. Told to pursue the safe and secure path.*
  - *Spending time alone*
  - *Take healthy risks*
  - *Desire to fix things – encourage them with kits*

## Takeaway #3
*Why our fears get worse as we age, and how to overcome them*

### Why we're afraid of tinkering:
- *Limiting beliefs about abilities and access to resources*
- *Myth of the 10,000 hours rule – we feel like we're already behind (Focus by Daniel Goleman)*
- *Afraid to take risks – we have to provide for ourselves and our families*

### How to overcome:
- *How to tinker and overcome our fear and keep it at bay from childhood to adulthood*
- *Story #3: Elaine Levin and the Podna Rover*

### Conclusion
- *Recap the three stories and the three takeaways.*
- *End with something like, "I hope you'll go out and tinker today!"*

## The importance of motivation and actionable takeaways

Before we move on, we want to underscore the importance of the motivation and takeaway sections above.

You've probably watched people who give really inspiring talks. Here's the thing: half the time you walk away amazed without a clue about what to do next. In the opposite scenario, you attend a how-to talk and walk away with action steps, but you don't feel motivated to do anything. Don't let your talk fall into either trap.

Let's start with the motivational issue first. No matter what your topic is, you'll always want to give your audience a high-level reason or sense of urgency for them to keep listening to your talk. Start by asking yourself, "Why is this important to my ideal audience?" Do this up front, before digging into takeaways.

For example, in Karen's 2014 TEDx talk, she spoke about how women are missing from the tech workforce and why this is a big problem. To get everyone's attention, she started the talk by sharing data about the number of tech workers that US businesses predict they'll need by 2022. Then she revealed the expected shortfall to demonstrate that we need more trained workers, both men and women. Next, she explained the importance of having diverse tech teams and why we need more women specifically.

Like Karen did, you can spend time on motivation at the start of your talk (we recommend doing this right after the introduction). But you can also provide extra motivation throughout your talk. Each time you introduce a new takeaway, you give the audience some urgency and a reason to pay attention to that particular lesson. This is a must if you're giving a long-form talk because it gives the audience a reason to stay engaged for a long time.

Then, transform this motivation into action. If you succeed in getting your audience amped up about an issue, what do you want them to do? Make sure your takeaways are insightful, memorable, and, ideally, actionable.

Consider whether you need to provide instructions. If your presentation is an educational how-to talk, you need to give very clear guidelines to help the audience implement your recommendations. Include a quick overview of an approach and break it down into a series of steps (we do this in the activities in this book). Make sure the steps are sequential and there are no gaps.

## Underlining a key message

Another way to make your talk memorable and actionable is to repeat a key phrase throughout your presentation to remind the audience about the underlying message. We call this "underlining."

In Karen's TEDx talk, her key message was that "we need more women to shape the future of technology." She stated it in the first few minutes and then repeated it as she layered on examples and stories. Then she ended the talk with a call-to-action to help encourage more women to get involved with the future of tech. She readily admits that she got sick of saying that phrase while she practiced the talk, but she knew it would make for a memorable takeaway. It was the one key message she hoped the audience would remember, if nothing else.

Beth Dunn uses this technique in her talk "How to Be a Writing God,"[20] at INBOUND, a content marketing conference. Halfway into her talk, she introduces her key message with a catchphrase: "Write like crap if you have to, but write every day." She repeats this message about six times with an accompanying visual on her slide deck to drive the point home. When she compares running practice to writing practice, she uses the message again: "I ran like crap every day, but I ran every day."

As you create your outline, think about whether there is a key message you can repeat over and over again throughout your talk. Mark places where you would reinforce it.

## Outline your stories

In Chapter 5, you found some stories to include in your talk; place them in the appropriate section in your main talk outline. It's also helpful to create sub-outlines for each story that you're including. This helps you crystallize the true value of the story, cut unnecessary details, and make sure the lesson comes across clearly to the audience.

Use the four stages of a story as your structure, and fill in bullets underneath each stage:

- Context

- Challenge

- Available solutions

- Final takeaway(s)

As an example, we'll outline the story of Elaine Levin from Poornima's TEDx talk above.

### Sample outline of Story #3: Elaine Levin

**Context**
- *People often lose interest in tinkering as they get older or face difficult health conditions.*
- *Their limiting beliefs make them feel like they:*
  - *have fallen behind the times*
  - *are afraid to take on risky new activities*
  - *have other obligations to family and friends*

- *Meet Elaine Levin.*
  - *Elaine is a sixty-three-year-old woman who suffers from multiple sclerosis.*
  - *She is losing mobility.*

### Challenge
- *Elaine wants to maintain an active lifestyle.*
- *There aren't great options out there. Can she create a solution for herself?*
- *Is it possible for someone in her situation to tinker?*
- *The problem is bigger than Elaine. Thousands are diagnosed with multiple sclerosis each year.*

### Available solutions

### Option 1
- *Elaine could use an existing mobility product like a walker, but they can be unstable.*

### Option 2 (This is the one she went with.)
- *Elaine could tinker; she could "scratch her own itch" and create a product for herself that would give her more freedom.*
- *She teamed up with a designer to create a new walker called the Podna Rover.*
- *She was awarded a patent in February 2010.*

### Final takeaways
- *You can tinker at any age. Elaine is a great example.*
- *Tip: Scratch your own itch and develop a product that solves a problem you know well.*

## Struggling? Use the Spill It Strategy

If you're stuck, try the Spill It Strategy, which helps you come up with good, conversational-sounding content for your talk. We recommend it for introductions, conclusions, and takeaways that are difficult to verbalize. It also helps you tell stories in a natural way.

In short, you just spill out all the knowledge in your head into spoken words, and then summarize them in your outline. Here's how to do it.

First, get an audio or video recorder. We recommend you record yourself so you can capture anything brilliant that you wouldn't want to forget. Next, put on your improvisation hat. Pick one takeaway or subject, forget everything else, and start talking about it.

This works best if you feel uninhibited. You'll draw interesting parallels and remember examples that you normally wouldn't. When you judge, you constrain your thinking (just like in a brainstorm). We strongly recommend you follow these rules to protect yourself from self-censorship:

- **Rule #1**
  As you're talking about each takeaway, don't worry about sounding logical or about your particular word choices, gestures, walking, pausing, transitions, who your audience is, or anything else you know about style or delivery.

- **Rule #2**
  Say the words out loud, not in your head.

- **Rule #3**
  When you go back and listen to your recording, do not judge yourself. Remember, this is just a brainstorming session.

Once you've gotten it all out, listen to your recording and draw out key phrases and lines of thought to populate your outline.

If you're still stuck on an area of your talk, you can revisit the Inventory Method from Chapter 3. You answered questions in five key areas to find a topic you can speak about with authority, and it can be helpful to try these again to get more content for your talk.

## Try answering them out loud this time and record them:

- **Question 1**
  What problems did you solve?

- **Question 2**
  What were your particular contributions?

- **Question 3**
  What were your challenges, and how did you overcome them?

- **Question 4**
  What did you learn, and how did you learn it?

- **Question 5**
  What's your advice to others in your shoes?

Are you ready to develop your own outline?

# PRACTICE

## OUTLINE YOUR TALK

First, take out a piece of paper or your computer. Keep your talk proposal handy to borrow bullet points related to takeaways and motivation.

Next, jot down subheadings for each main section of your talk in the order provided below. Add supporting bullet points with information you want to provide like stats and quotes, aiming for an outline about one page long. You'll pare this down as you practice, but for now, it's okay to be detailed.

1. **Introduction**
   Include an introduction
   (e.g., you might open with your story).

2. **Motivation**
   Provide some motivation to listen to the talk and preview the takeaways (or benefits) the audience will walk away with. It can be helpful to review the summary and takeaways you wrote in your talk proposal.

3. **Takeaways**
   Create a subsection for each takeaway in your talk proposal (e.g., Takeaway 1, Takeaway 2, Takeaway 3).

# PRACTICE CONTINUED

4. **Conclusion**

Create a conclusion. This can include a final statement, a recap of the takeaways, and/or a call-to-action.

5. **Next, add one or more stories**

Outline each one with bullet points using these stages of a story. (Refer to Chapter 5 if you need a refresher or an activity to guide you.)

- Context

- Challenge

- Available solutions

6. **Final takeaway(s)**

Jot each story down underneath the section where you will tell it; or, if you're using the **Slow Reveal Technique,** bullet out which details you'll reveal in each section.

You can use the "underlining" technique to reinforce your key message. Summarize the message into a short phrase and mark a few places in your outline where you can repeat it.

# RECAP

## CHAPTER 7

### Outline your talk, but don't create a script

Outlining your talk is a fast way to organize content and gives you more mastery over your material than a script does.

Create an outline with the following sections:

1. Introduction
2. Motivation
3. Takeaways
4. Conclusion

Try the **Spill It Strategy** to brainstorm content and find ideas to support your main points.

# 8
## PRACTICE

Now it's time to practice. Practice serves two critical functions: it helps you edit your talk content and makes your delivery smooth.

This is a natural continuation of the outline work you did in Chapter 7. You'll speak through your outline for the first time by explaining your outline out loud. This helps you notice areas that you can cut, that sound unnatural, or that need a few more supporting ideas. You'll go back to your outline to make changes, then practice it out loud again, repeating the process until the talk meets the target length and flows well.

When you feel comfortable with your content, practice it. You'll eventually be able to deliver your talk without notes.

Many people don't realize they need to practice in front of others to simulate the conditions of a real talk. This helps tackle the unique emotions and presentation habits that arise when you get in front of a group. We'll teach our favorite practice method, which involves both one-on-one and group scenarios. It works wonders for confidence and gives you a chance to ask for feedback on your talk and delivery style.

Don't skip practicing. The most natural presenters (who seem like they wake up in the morning with a microphone in hand) all have something in common: they prepare.

Even Steve Jobs needed to practice. Carmine Gallo, who wrote *The Presentation Secrets of Steve Jobs: How to Be Insanely Great in Front of Any Audience*, reported that "Steve Jobs cannot pull off an intricate presentation with video clips, demonstrations, and outside speakers without hours of rehearsal. I have spoken to people within Apple who tell me that Jobs rehearses the entire presentation aloud for many hours. Nothing is taken for granted."[21]

Before practicing your final talk, we need to finish developing your talk content by speaking through it out loud for the first time.

## Talk through your outline out loud

You've come a long way in the development of your talk. You've considered your audience, found the main takeaways - the "gifts" - that you want to convey, and created an outline of the supporting messages that will convey them.

Your outline isn't complete yet. You need to explain each section of your outline out loud to reveal things you can't spot when jotting down bullet points. Once you do this, you'll cut pieces of the outline, move sections, and add embellishments through repeated practice.

Yes, you need to do this out loud. Saying the words in your head does not count.

Why? Because the way you speak and deliver a talk is very different from the way you would say the words in your head. When you say the words in your head, you're perfect. You don't slur your speech, you don't say "um" and "uh," and you certainly don't trip over your own words.

But when you deliver your talk out loud, you'll make mistakes. It's only natural. So we recommend saying the words out loud whenever you practice, even from the very beginning.

When you hear yourself out loud, two things happen:

- You start to spot sentences that sound awkward.
- You notice logical errors.

Your ears have been trained for many years to spot these two issues, so put them to use.

The first run-through certainly doesn't need to be formal. And don't worry about talk length or tempo yet. Just look at your outline, take a deep breath, and start speaking.

You can do this alone, but if you find it daunting to start talking through your outline for the first time – and many people who are new to public speaking do – then schedule some time with a good friend and bring your outline to them. Sit right next to them and simply talk through the whole outline, explaining it to them person to person. It'll help you present information casually and get used to saying the words out loud.

When you've completed this, start back at the top and speak through your outline several more times. For your first two or three practice rounds, you may feel like it takes a long time to get through your outline, and this is okay. Focus on the content and clarity of your explanations.

Once you get a bit more comfortable, set a stopwatch and speak the outline out loud one more time to get a baseline reading of your talk length. (Instead of setting a countdown timer for your target length – for example, five minutes for a five-minute lightning talk – we recommend you use a stopwatch that counts up from zero to get an accurate recording of how long it takes you to get through your entire talk.) And don't feel like you need to rush through or worry about timing just yet. You'll make sure the talk content fits your time constraints in the next section, and you'll also pick up speed once you get familiar with your content.

Speaking your outline out loud is an important milestone, so use this guide to do it before you move to the next section.

# PRACTICE
## TALK THROUGH YOUR OUTLINE

*Involves other people (optional).*

Speak through your talk outline as if you were explaining each section to a friend, filling in details as you go.

1. **(Optional) Find a friend to help**
   Explaining each section of your outline to a friend can help you get through your first run-through out loud. Sit down with a friend in a private place where you can focus. (You can do this step alone if you prefer, however.)

2. **Look at your outline and start to talk through it**
   Starting with the introduction, read each section and explain it out loud, hitting all the main points you outlined.

   - Take as long as you like. Aim to give clear explanations and to find comfort with your material rather than going quickly.

   - Don't worry about your stance, gestures, inflections, or what slide you might like to display during a section.

# PRACTICE CONTINUED

3. **Repeat one or two more times slowly**

    Once you get to the end of your outline, take a break and then go back to the top to repeat it one or two more times.

    Pay attention to what works, what doesn't, what needs more details, and what doesn't need as many details as you've provided.

4. **Time yourself**

    Set a stopwatch and talk through your outline one more time slowly. Don't look at the clock; you're not racing, but instead getting a baseline reading of the length. Continue to aim for clarity and comfort with the material.

## Making the cut

Most outlines have far more content than you can fit into your talk's time constraints, so you'll have to discard some of it.

The first step is to know how much you need to cut. In the previous section, you timed your entire talk using a stopwatch. Compare how much time it took you to run through your talk with your target talk length. Then, go back to your outline and think about what you want to cut.

If you like, you can tackle the cuts one section of your talk at a time to make the exercise more manageable and to ensure your talk has an even cadence. Use a stopwatch while you speak through your outline again, and mark the time at which you move from one section to the next (you can also have a friend take notes while you focus on your material). Then, give each section a time "target." For example, if your goal is to deliver a five-minute lightning talk, you'll need to make sure you're not spending more than sixty seconds on the introduction, roughly ninety seconds on each takeaway, and thirty to sixty seconds to review and conclude.

(For specific help on adapting your talk content to formats like five-minute lightning talks and long-form talks greater than thirty minutes, see Chapters 16 and 17, respectively).

Revisit your outline and remove anything that's not crucial to your main points. Stories can drain time, so remove extraneous details. If you tell a story in your introduction that's so long it tips the talk out of balance, consider spreading out the story sections throughout your talk with the Slow Reveal Technique from Chapter 5. If you need to reduce your time drastically, consider removing an entire story or a takeaway.

Make cuts and speak through your outline, repeating as many times as needed until you're at a good talk length. Then, put your notes away.

## Pay attention to transitions

Notice how you transition between subjects as you speak through your outline out loud. As you progress from one topic to another, usher the audience along smoothly with phrases like these:

- **Counterpoint transitions**
  If the next point is counter to the one before it, you can say something like, "On the other hand..." or "However..."

- **Supporting point transitions**
  If the next point is an extension of the previous one, you can say something like, "Moreover..." or "Let's dig into this deeper..."

- **Standalone point transitions**
  Sometimes you have points that stand alone and don't have a strong connection to each other. In that case, it's okay to signal a complete change using phrases like, "Let's switch gears..." or "Let's move on and talk about..."

To give each transition bigger impact, pause beforehand. This gives your audience a chance to think about your previous point and creates a professional-sounding pace.

## Clarify jargon

This phase is also a good time to add clarifications for industry jargon and acronyms, especially if you're presenting to an audience of varying job functions and levels of expertise.

People prefer listening to someone who uses simple, compelling language; that doesn't mean you can never use jargon, and sometimes it's necessary or more efficient to do so. If you do, just make sure that everyone in the audience knows what you're talking about. Even if you think that more than half of the audience knows a term, you should still take a quick moment to explain it.

For example, you might say, "Many of you already know what a histogram is, but just in case some of you aren't familiar with it, I'm going to take a minute to explain how to use a histogram to visualize big data."

With this approach, you're just acknowledging that it's natural for people to have varying levels of experience with a concept and taking a moment to get everyone on the same page.

## Ready? Wean yourself off the outline

Now that you've run through your outline plenty of times, you're ready to set the outline aside while you speak through your talk again. If this sounds scary, know that it'll get easier with practice.
You might be tempted to use an index card with cues, but keeping something in your hand cripples your presentation: you're not as free to gesture, you'll look down at it and avoid eye contact, and you'll always be concerned with what comes next.

Instead, you want to hold your main points in your head and be able to speak about them freely.

Force yourself to talk through your outline without looking at it. We guarantee that you will trip up often at first. You'll forget your lines, you'll pick words that sound strange, and you'll probably be worried about your body language. It's going to feel weird, like riding a bike without training wheels for the first time.

But keep practicing without notes, and you'll improve quickly.

## Get By with a Little Help from Your Friends

A great way to practice a talk is the **Get By with a Little Help from Your Friends Method**. It's our favorite method, and we always go through this technique in full for each talk we give. In fact, we often repeat the process a few times as we incorporate feedback and change our talk.

The first step in this technique is to speak your talk out loud and practice by yourself until you don't need an outline - if you've followed the process in this chapter so far, you've already done this step. The next three steps get progressively similar to real presentation conditions.

Try to complete all the steps in order to refine your content; you'll get feedback from others that may change your talk. Your goal is to get to a point where you're confident that your content is helpful, you're meeting time constraints, and you can remember your main points easily.

Only when you've reached that stage is it time to improve your delivery style through your voice, movements, body language, and even slides. Once you introduce these elements, we recommend that you revisit the Get By with a Little Help from Your Friends Method to practice again.

Here's how it goes:

- **Step 1: Practice by yourself**
  (If you've practiced the techniques in this chapter so far, you've completed Step 1.) Speak your talk out loud. Depending on how far you are in your talk development

process, you can speak from an outline and eventually wean yourself off your notes.

- **Step 2: Practice in front of a camera, recording your presentation**
  Set up a camera or laptop, stand in front of it, and record yourself giving your talk without notes.

  Play it back and watch for any strange gestures. You don't need to be overly critical; you just need to be aware, and your mind will automatically correct this behavior the next time you run through your talk. We know it seems a little strange, but it does work.

  You can also keep track of time and pay attention to how long you're spending on the introduction, takeaways, and conclusion. If you notice that the time isn't spread out evenly among sections, then make adjustments to your talk.

- **Step 3: Practice with one other person**
  Get your best friend, significant other, or coworker to watch a practice run. This step helps you sound conversational because it's easier to have a conversation with one person than with an audience. Ask them to time you. You can also have them provide feedback on your talk content. If they aren't familiar with the topic, they can still comment on your overall style, poise, and gestures.

- **Step 4: Practice with a mini-audience**
  Round up a group of three to five people or more. They can be friends, family, or colleagues. Make sure at least a couple of them are knowledgeable about your talk's topic and can provide useful feedback on your presentation's content.

## How to assemble a mini-audience for the Get By with a Little Help from Your Friends Method

Step 4 of the method – speaking in front of a mini-audience of friends and colleagues – is so useful that we want to make sure you do it. Don't skip over it just because you may feel intimidated or because it takes extra work to assemble people.

Here's a step-by-step guide, complete with email request templates, to make the process a little less painful.

# PRACTICE
## ASSEMBLE YOUR MINI-AUDIENCE

Find your audience. Make a list of three to five supportive people in your network in front of whom you can practice at least once.

Invite them to your practice talk. Invite them to watch you practice your talk and ask them for feedback. Make it fun! Tempt them with homemade baked goods or invite them over to dinner and then present your talk. If people can't attend an in-person meeting, ask whether they would be open to joining via videoconferencing or watching a recording.

Here's an email template as a starting point.

### Email template for your mini-audience

> *Subject: Need your feedback on an upcoming talk*
>
> *Hi {First name},*
>
> *Hope you're having a good day!*
>
> *I'm creating a talk for {event or situation}, and my next step is to practice speaking in front of a few people in order to become comfortable speaking to groups and to collect feedback.*

# PRACTICE CONTINUED

*I'd like to invite you to be a member of my mini-audience so you can watch my talk and share suggestions.*

*All I need is thirty minutes of your time on {suggest date and time}.*

*Does that work for you?*

*Kindly,*
*{Your name}*

## Incorporating peer feedback

When you present in front of a friend and a mini-audience, ask them to provide feedback on your content and eventually on your delivery style.

A word of warning: It can be hard to stay focused when your mini-audience is scribbling notes about your presentation. You may start second-guessing your talk or get distracted as you wonder what they wrote down. When Karen practiced her TEDx talk in front of Poornima and a few other friends, she vividly remembers Poornima taking about four pages of notes, and frankly, it was intimidating. If this happens to you, just remember that some of your audience's notes will be about how awesome your talk is.

Also, beware of the "feedback frenzy." You don't need to incorporate each and every suggestion. Think through critiques before slashing content or adding to your presentation, considering whether a statement supports or detracts from your core message, and using your gut instinct about what will resonate with your target audience.

Sometimes your friends will suggest many additions to your talk, pushing you over the time limit. A great way to combat a rapidly expanding presentation is to ask them what they recommend you cut in order to incorporate their ideas. They might back down on some points. And of course, any time you make a big change, make sure it reflects the needs of your ideal audience member and that you time yourself doing the presentation again.

Congratulations; if you've completed Part II, you've created a talk. Your next step is to hone your delivery style (and then, of course, practice again). Parts III and IV give you ways to make your content shine and handle tricky presentation situations. Before your big day, make sure to review Chapter 14, which provides tips on day-of logistical details.

# RECAP

## CHAPTER 8

### Refine your talk content by speaking through your talk outline

Bring your talk to life by reading through and explaining your outline out loud. Repeat until you meet your talk's time target and can speak through it without looking at notes. Then, practice until your delivery is smooth.

### Practice with the Get By with a Little Help from Your Friends Method

1. Practice by yourself.

2. Practice in front of a camera, recording your presentation.

3. Practice with one other person.

4. Practice with a mini-audience.

### Don't forget to ask for feedback!

# PART III
## DELIVER LIKE A PRO

If you've worked through Part II, congratulations: you have a talk on your hands. Now that you've nailed down your content, Part III helps you polish your delivery style.

The first thing we'll tackle is stage fright. Many of our students experience stage fright, and nearly everyone gets a bit nervous before speaking. (Yes, we get nervous too.) We recommend that you read through Chapter 9 and try our techniques no matter how you feel about public speaking, because they'll improve your confidence dramatically.

In Chapter 10, you'll learn eight ways to use your body and voice to make your delivery pop, as well as classic mistakes to avoid because they detract from your presentation. Experimenting with your speaking style is fun and helps you find what feels authentic, and this is key to feeling confident onstage.

Chapter 11 shows you how to build slides the easy way and make sure they accent your talk, not distract from it.

Make sure to practice your talk again when you decide to incorporate new delivery styles. You can go back to the Get By with a Little Help from Your Friends Method in Chapter 8 as many times as you need to before presentation day.

# 9

# GET OVER STAGE FRIGHT

You know your material, you've laid out your talk, and you can speak through it without looking at notes. Still nervous? It's time to tackle the toughest topic of them all: the fear of public speaking.

Stage fright can feel crippling, whether you're a beginner or experienced. Even professional speakers, performers, and celebrities – from Prince Harry to Barbra Streisand – admit to their fear of the spotlight.

Stage fright is absolutely manageable, and with a few techniques you'll feel much more comfortable giving talks. And there's a difference between stage fright and nerves. Everyone gets nerves, especially right before speaking, so it helps to expect that you'll get them and to know that it's not a real threat.

For example, even though we have long track records as professional public speakers, we felt anxious before our TEDx talks.

I was worried for weeks leading up to my talk. I diligently planned my outline and created my slides. I practiced in front of my computer and my family, and I worked with a speech coach. I also did a trial run with a mini-audience to get feedback. With each passing day, the knot in my stomach grew heavier. I kept thinking, "What the heck have I signed myself up for?"

*Like Karen, I practiced my talk by myself, with a speech coach, with my family, and with friends. I was feeling pretty great the day before and the day of the talk.*

*But once they told me it was time to go onstage, I started to feel that pit in my stomach, and it only got worse. As I was walking, I got really nervous. I finally reached the red circle that they put on the stage for TEDx speakers to stand on, and my knees were shaking.*

The good thing is, pre-presentation nerves often calm down once you start speaking. We had the time of our lives giving our TEDx talks once we got over our initial worries and felt the thrill of giving a good presentation.

First, we'll look at why stage fright happens to both beginners and experts and how you can get in a better mindset. Then, we'll share our favorite techniques to squash stage fright and calm nerves.

## Stage fright is human

If you're afraid to get onstage, you're in good company. It's only human. One natural cause of stage fright is our survival instinct. We are evolutionarily predisposed to hide from predators and find shelter to secure ourselves. In the wide open, we are more vulnerable, so standing exposed in front of a group or on a spacious stage goes against our biological tendencies. If you perspire, your heart beats a little faster, or you get red in the face, it's helpful to remember that these reactions are common and automatic.

Being human also means there's a possibility that something about your talk won't go perfectly. You might be afraid of failure: people might reject your ideas, the crowd's response might disappoint you, or you might embarrass yourself with a slipup.

## Are you giving *yourself* stage fright?

Negative thought patterns can exacerbate your anxiety about giving presentations. Here are four of the most common ones. Do you experience any of these? Identifying and naming negative thought patterns is the first step toward correcting them.

- **Pattern #1: You psych yourself into thinking that you will get stage fright.**
Is your fear a self-fulfilling prophecy that becomes true by the very nature of the belief?

If you go into a public speaking situation thinking, "I'm going to get stage fright," then you're going to interpret the slightest signs of sweaty palms and anxiety as the precursors to full-blown stage fright. This negative thought confirms your belief: "Yep, see? It's already starting. I can feel sweat on my hands. I'm definitely going to have a panic attack. There's no way around it." In reality, a raised heartbeat or a flutter in your stomach might predict the onset of full-blown stage fright, but it doesn't have to.

- **Pattern #2: You want to be perfect.**
Holding yourself to unachievable standards is a surefire way to cause anxiety. And it's unnecessary. The key to excellent public speaking is confidence, not perfection.

As you learn to embrace mistakes and move past them, the stage will become less and less scary. Dale Carnegie, a prolific teacher of public speaking in the US during the twentieth century and author of *The Art of Public*

*Speaking,*[22] once said, "First ask yourself: What is the worst that can happen? Then prepare to accept it. Then proceed to improve on the worst."

- **Pattern #3: You are your own worst critic.**
  Another one of our favorite quotes from Dale Carnegie sums up this idea well: "There are always three speeches for every one you actually gave. The one you practiced, the one you gave, and the one you wish you gave."

The audience doesn't have access to the speech you practiced, nor to the speech you wish you gave, so they can't compare them to your real performance. You don't need to either!

When Poornima finished her TEDx talk, she felt that she performed so-so and was a little disappointed. She was surprised when people from the audience approached her afterward and told her how much they got out of the presentation. It became clear that she was more critical than she needed to be.

Self-critical thoughts only exacerbate stage fright, so combat them with a reality check and remember that you're probably harsher on yourself than anyone else will be.

- **Pattern #4: You focus on the wrong things.**
  On presentation day, you might be worried about your hair, how you're going to sound on the recording of your talk, or if you're like us, that spot of salsa from lunch on your white shirt. But your audience only cares about how clear and compelling you are. They want to be educated and entertained, not to critique your fashion choices.

Focus on them, not on yourself.

As Karen prepped for her TEDx talk, she told her speech coach that she wanted to do a great job to help build her personal brand. This was her priority; after all, the video would be posted on the TED YouTube channel, which would be great exposure. The coach gently chastised her. She recommended that Karen's goal be to inspire people to follow her call-to-action. By changing her focus from her professional agenda to her mission to convince the audience, Karen became more passionate about giving her talk, which in turn allowed her to shine on the day of the talk and in the video.

It's natural to be stressed about details like your appearance or how the talk will increase your professional street cred, and unfortunately, that's only going to make you more nervous. Remember that the audience won't care about those things. They want to learn from you and be inspired by you.

## Six techniques to help you overcome stage fright

Here are the techniques that work for us and for the students we've coached. Try them out as you read, or return to them once you've finished the chapter or are practicing for a talk. Be open-minded and notice whether you resist or have resistant thoughts:

- "I'm just not cut out for this..."
- "I already know this..."
- "This won't work for me..."

If you're skeptical about the techniques or aren't worried about stage fright, try our methods anyway while you prepare for your next presentation. You may surprise yourself when you feel calmer than you expected, or when a trick you already know becomes more powerful with practice.

### Technique #1: Strike a power pose

Strike a power pose for just two minutes in order to feel strong, confident, powerful, and less nervous.

- **What is a power pose?**

  Think about what athletes tend to do when they've just won their event. They raise their arms in victory. You see it at the Olympics when a runner crosses the finish line or at a youth soccer game when a player kicks the ball into the goal. When we have power, we use our body language to show it. And get this: we can use body language to fake it 'til we make it.

- **How does this work?**

  Research by Dana Carney, Amy Cuddy, and Andy Yap[23] shows that striking a power pose for just two minutes raises our testosterone levels and makes us feel strong and dominant. At the same time, it reduces our stress by lowering cortisol. To learn more, watch Amy Cuddy's popular TED talk, "Your Body Language Shapes Who You Are."[24]

Try this before you give a talk, or to calm your nerves before an important meeting, interview, or negotiation. You can even use it before asking a question during someone else's talk in a large auditorium.

Here are a few great power poses:

- Raise your arms in victory like an athlete who has just won.

- Pretend you are Wonder Woman, Superwoman, or your favorite superhero and put your hands or fists on your hips.

- Strike your favorite bodybuilding pose. Flex some muscles.

---

*Figure 9.1*

Now it's time to practice. Pick somewhere safe and comfortable, like your bedroom or a private conference room at work. Stand up and try the poses, holding each one for two minutes. Watch yourself in a mirror and pay attention to how you feel. You might feel silly at first, but it's worth it.

We love power poses. Karen used them in her hotel room the morning of her TEDx talk, and again in the restroom backstage at the conference. To her surprise, she wasn't nervous at all when it was time to step on the stage. She loved giving her talk and had fun. Poornima only learned about power poses from Karen after she gave her TEDx presentation, but she has been practicing them ever since, no matter how confident she thinks she is.

### Technique #2: Relax your body

Take five to ten deep breaths before you get on the stage, and take one more big one before you start saying your first few words. This helps your body relax and your mind become clear and focused. (Just make sure not to take that deep breath directly into the mic.)

It's harder to calm your breathing when your heart is racing from stimulants. So while you might think that getting hopped up on caffeine will help you stay alert and energetic, it can cause you to get more anxious than necessary. If you're concerned about having energy during the talk, skip coffee and invest in a good night's sleep for two nights before the talk.

### Technique #3: Release stress by interlocking fingers

If nerves are getting the best of you just before a talk, connect your thumbs and pointer fingers in interlocking circles, then pull back your hands. We don't know why it works, but it does!

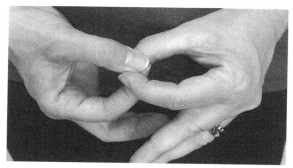

*Figure 9.2*

You can also clasp your thumbs in the opposite hands' palms and give them a hug. Check out more relaxing finger and hand positions like Jin Shin Jyutsu finger mudras.[25]

### Technique #4: Meet and greet the audience before you go onstage

If you're about to give a talk and have some time before going onstage, take advantage of the opportunity to mingle with guests. It brings your focus to your audience and how you can help them, leaving less room for inward-facing, anxiety-provoking thought patterns.

 *I recently delivered the keynote for a conference. I got to the auditorium with plenty of time to spare, and after connecting my laptop to the projection system, I started to pull out my phone to check my email. Then I realized I had an opportunity to say hello to the dozen or so*

*early birds who were already seated in the auditorium. I put my phone away, grabbed my business cards, and walked around, introducing myself and explaining that I would be giving the keynote. I asked people where they were from and what they did. By staying busy before going onstage, I kept my nerves at bay. I also felt I had a few new friends out there who would be rooting for me during my talk.*

Prepare some questions before your event to help break the ice. Here are some examples:

**Ice breaker #1**
*Hi, I'm Poornima, and I'll be moderating the panel. Thanks for coming. How did you hear about the event?*

**Ice breaker #2**
*Hi, I'm Karen, and I'll be speaking about diversity in the tech industry. Does your company have diversity initiatives underway?*

**Ice breaker #3**
*Hi, I'm Poornima. Thanks for taking the time to attend my talk. I'm curious, what's one thing you're hoping to get out of this presentation?*

### Technique #5: Practice
You knew we were going to say that, didn't you?

Practice is a powerful anti-anxiety technique and a step you should not skip. Most people think that the best speakers just wing it, but the truth is that professional speakers who are really polished always practice their talk before they deliver it.

You should practice alone to get comfortable with the material. You should practice in front of a camera to force yourself to speak your words out loud. And you should practice with a friend and with a small group to get their feedback. These are all critical confidence boosters. Chapter 8 explains in depth how to practice effectively.

### Technique #6: Identify and name specific anxieties

If you can identify specific stressors that make you anxious, you can mitigate them and even avoid them altogether to decrease your general anxiety level.

For example, each time we lead our public speaking workshop, our students voice concerns about an audience member asking them a question they can't answer. It's a significant cause of their stage fright and holds many of them back from giving talks.

If you're worried about getting a tough question, like these students do, acknowledge that Q&A is an issue and then try specialized remedies like practicing the Q&A-handling strategies in Chapter 12. Here are some more examples of specific anxieties from our students, as well as their ideas for solutions:

- **An audience member leaving during my talk**
  I worry that I'll blame my performance if someone leaves during my talk, causing me to lose my stage presence. One idea is to hold a positive explanation in my mind, like, "Oh, they probably just left for the restroom."

- **Being asked a question I don't know**
  My go-to method is to tell the audience member that I'll get back to them, but this hasn't done much to calm my fear, because I still feel like a deer in the headlights and I don't want to give my fallback response for multiple questions in the same session. One thing I could do in the future is to

prepare for a set of common questions ahead of time to reduce the chance that I'll get a series of "I don't know" questions. I could practice my talk in front of a couple of coworkers, ask them to think of as many questions as possible, write their ideas down, and prepare some answers in advance.

- **Arriving late**
  If it's a local event, then I check traffic, plan alternate routes, and do my best to get there thirty minutes early. It works for me already. I could always shoot to arrive one hour early if it's a talk I'm extra nervous about.

- **Slides not showing up properly**
  I ask the organizer if they support Keynote. Then when I arrive at the venue, I connect my computer and test my slides. It works most of the time. Next time, I could create backup versions of my slides in different file formats or test slides on-site a day early.

What are the things that make you feel anxious about public speaking? And what can you do to address each one? This technique is powerful, so here's an activity to guide you through the process.

# PRACTICE
## TACKLE SPECIFIC ANXIETIES

Identify and name things that trigger anxiety about giving a talk, then brainstorm ways to mitigate each one.

1. **Identify triggers**
   Start by creating a list of things that make you anxious about public speaking. Don't hold back; list anything and everything that comes to mind. (Examples include having an audience member leave, being asked a question you don't know the answer to, arriving late, having issues with slides, or getting criticism from the audience.)

2. **Brainstorm solutions**
   Next to each item on the list, complete the following tasks:

   • Explain any methods you've tried in the past to mitigate the worry or prevent the issue, or make a note if you haven't tried anything.

   • Reflect on whether the method has or hasn't worked for you in the past.

   • Jot down two to five ideas to help you tackle the trigger.

# RECAP
## CHAPTER 9

**Stage fright is common and natural**

Basic human instincts trigger the butterflies you get in your stomach when you step onstage. But there's a difference between stage fright and nervousness. True fear can be overcome, while pre-talk nerves happen to almost everyone – even experienced speakers.

**Try these techniques to get over stage fright and reduce nerves:**

- Strike a power pose
- Calm your body
- Release stress by interlocking fingers
- Meet and greet the audience before you go onstage
- Practice
- Identify and name specific anxieties

# 10
## STYLE YOUR TALK

What you say in your presentation is important, but how you say it makes all the difference.

Learn how to use your body and voice to convey messages clearly and keep your audience engaged. People will have an easier time following along, feel entertained, and remember your talk's takeaways.

A speaking style can become a professional signature, and we see this often in public figures. Stephen Colbert's style is deadpan. Steve Jobs was to the point, keeping statements short and sweet. He would often say, "One last thing," and the audience knew what was coming next – something big. Brené Brown is very casual, which makes the audience feel relaxed and that they can relate to her.

But there is no one "right" speaking style, and you don't need to copy someone's style just because he or she is a successful speaker. Use them as inspiration, but don't force yourself to mimic them, because that could clash with your authentic voice and feel unnatural.

Try many techniques. When you find what feels authentic, you'll not only look confident onstage, but you'll feel more comfortable too. Having fun will give you motivation to take on more, better, and bigger speaking opportunities in the future, so if you're serious about speaking, experimenting with style is a worthwhile investment.

Your style will evolve throughout your career and may even change from talk to talk. For example, you might enjoy using dramatic vocal techniques and big gestures in front of an audience of peers and feel more comfortable being serious when presenting to your boss's boss.

Here are eight ways to engage an audience with your body and voice. We'll dive into each one and provide an activity at the end of the chapter to help you try out some techniques.

- Body language
- Eye contact
- Gestures
- Walking
- Vocal inflections
- Enunciation
- Speed
- Volume and pitch

## Body language

Body language is a powerful form of nonverbal communication. It can convey confidence and openness. When you "close yourself off" with your body, you appear small and defensive, like you're hiding something or hiding from something. Open body language, on the other hand, projects confidence and welcomes people in.

When you present, do you close your body off by making these classic mistakes?

- **Closing your stance**
  When you cross your arms, put hands in your pockets, or hold a notebook, you block people from seeing your body. These movements can be fleeting and unconscious, so to figure out whether you do this, record yourself practicing a talk or have a friend observe.

- **Using a lectern**
  Lecterns (tall reading desks with slanted tops that are installed on some stages, often in universities and churches) were originally designed to hold books and notes. But we no longer hold books while presenting, and should avoid using notes. Unless the lectern has an attached mic that you need to use, don't stand behind it. It's tempting to seek physical protection from it, but it will hide more than half of your body (especially if you're petite like Poornima) and send a message to the audience that you are distant and closed off from them.

- **Using a microphone stand**
  When you stand in front of a mic, you obstruct the audience's view of you and limit your movement. If it's possible, ask the event host to provide a headset mic or a clip-on lavalier mic to allow you to walk about freely.

*Figure 10.1*

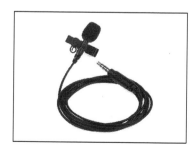

*Figure 10.2*

- **Turning your back to the audience**
  If you turn your back to the audience – for example, to look at your slides – you close your body off and break the link between you and your listeners.

## Eye contact

You'll also damage your connection with the audience if you conspicuously avoid looking at your audience members – for example, if your eyes are looking at the floor, roving around the ceiling and walls, or trained on your slides. When you're presenting to small and midsized audiences, eye contact can strengthen your relationship with the audience. It reminds you to stay conversational when you present.

Here's how to pull it off. Meet someone's eyes and hold contact for fifteen to thirty seconds. Then, break contact as you shift to meeting the eyes of another person in the room. You can synchronize these transitions with subject transitions so that one person gets a complete thought before you move on to the next. If fifteen to thirty seconds feels long to you at first, start with ten seconds and work your way up.

Don't jump wildly from one side of the room to the other, but slowly sweep across it, making sure to connect with people in the fringes and at the back of the room. And don't stare at just one person, because this can make them uncomfortable or make you forget about the others. It's easier than you think to accidentally focus too much attention on one person, especially if you're nervous and they are reassuring to you (e.g., because you know them personally or because they're smiling and nodding).

If you're presenting to an audience of hundreds, you may have a harder time making direct eye contact with people. Lisa B. Marshall, host of *The Public Speaker* podcast,[26] suggests that you look in the "sweet spot" two-thirds of the way deep into an auditorium, toward the center; at this distance, most people in the audience will think you're looking at them.

When you take a question during Q&A, make eye contact with the person asking the question at the start of your answer, then move on to other people in the audience so they are included as well. When you end your response, bring it full circle and make eye contact with the original audience member again to confirm that they understood your answer.

## Gestures

Gestures are attention grabbing. Humans are wired to detect and process motion immediately. Gestures can accompany the auditory part of your talk to provide some visual stimulation, but they play important roles in helping your audience follow along with you and pay attention to the most important points in your presentation.

Here are three ways you can use gestures to accompany your talk. To get a better idea of what each gesture looks like, check out the corresponding videos in the ★ Present! interactive bundle.

- **Signposting**
  Signposting helps your audience keep track of where you are in a list. For example, you might present five steps in a process, two examples that support a point, or three key takeaways. You can count out each point in the list on your fingers by raising them up when you move to the next point. This gives your audience a clear signal that you are transitioning.

For example, you might say, "Step 1 [raise 1 finger], preheat the oven to 350 degrees. Step 2 [raise 2 fingers], assemble your ingredients. Step 3 [raise 3 fingers]..."

*Figure 10.3*

*Figure 10.4*

- **Giving your audience cues**
  When you want your audience to perform a certain action, you can use a change in your body language to get them to pay attention or gear up to act.

  For example, if you want to take a quick poll of the audience by asking for a show of hands, raise your own hand as you pose the question. This might sound like, "[raise your hand] Show of hands: How many of you have used an open source framework before?"

  Here's another example. When you ask the audience a question, real or rhetorical, take a step forward and lean toward them. This gesture helps the audience pay attention and shift gears internally to answer your question in their minds.

- **Mirroring**
  When your gestures mirror what you're talking about, they provide a visual emphasis.

For example, if you say something like "narrowed" or "limited," bring your hands in. If you say "widened," then spread them out. Do the same with "big" and "small."

If you have a series of points that follow one another (like cause and effect), or you're talking about an event that progresses over time, move your hand along a line rather than keeping it in the same spot.

Gestures add to your talk, but too much movement can detract in some cases.

First, some speakers are too repetitive with their gestures, like bouncing one hand up and down or walking back and forth nonstop. Most of the time, this is because repetitive movement helps them keep pace and feels natural to them (or they're just nervous). Unfortunately, it is distracting to the audience and can make them miss what you're trying to say.

Make sure to do the activity at the end of this chapter, in which you'll record yourself speaking in front of a camera and then watch the playback. Look for any repetitive gestures that are distracting and try to limit them the next time you record yourself or give a talk. As strange as it might feel, it's totally okay to keep your arms at your sides and relax from time to time.

Remote control slide clickers can cause more distracting movements, but it's common to use a clicker to run through presentation slides. So if you use one, make sure you keep it in the same hand throughout your talk. Don't play with it. Avoid using a handheld mic at the same time as a clicker so that you can have one hand free for gesturing – opt for a headset or lavalier mic instead.

## Walking

You can stand in one spot during your talk, but why not use the physical space around you to keep the audience even more visually engaged?

One of our favorite walking techniques is to move across a space in one progressive direction to mark moments in time. For example, if you're talking about three stages of your career, imagine dividing the stage into three sections. Standing at stage right, talk about your early career. Then, walk to center stage to talk about what you were doing mid-career. Walk to stage left to talk about what you're doing now, in your later career. Your position on the stage becomes a marker for where you are in your story, which helps the audience stay focused and remember its points.

You can also strategically move toward the audience to show sincerity or honesty, which lets them see you close up with nothing to hide. Monica Lewinsky did exactly this in her recent TED talk about shaming and what happened to her after her relationship with former President Bill Clinton became public.[27] Toward the end of her talk, she addressed why she was coming forward at this time, just before presidential candidates would be announcing their intentions to run. She stepped sideways, away from the music stand that held her notes, and took a couple of steps toward the audience. She then explained that the timing of her talk was not for political reasons. Those strategic steps sent a strong message that she was being sincere.

## Vocal inflections

Another way to keep the audience engaged with the content of your talk is to vary the tone of your voice. Tone depicts emotion and action, which elicits emotional responses and increased attention from your audience members.

If you don't use vocal inflections, then your talk will be monotonous, which bores your audience and can even put them to sleep, like white noise that is just loud enough to drown out background noise and lull listeners into dreamland.

Here are three types of vocal inflections. To make it a little easier to understand what we're talking about, we recommend watching the video clips we've included in the ★ Present! interactive bundle. After you do this, try saying the examples below out loud:

## Upward inflection

Change your vocal pitch from a lower to a higher note during a vowel sound. This change in pitch indicates questioning, insincerity, surprise, or suspense.

- *"Maybe?"*
  When your voice uses an upward inflection with "maybe," it signifies questioning.

- *"No, really?"*
  This can indicate questioning or surprise.

## Downward inflection

Change your vocal pitch from a higher to a lower note during a vowel sound. This change in pitch indicates confidence, finality, power, and certainty.

- *"Maybe."*
  When you use a downward inflection with "maybe," it indicates power.

- *"Done." "No." "Go."*
  When your voice drops when you say "done" and "no," you'll convey certainty and confidence. A command like "go," with a downward inflection, sounds powerful.

**Level inflection**
Don't change your pitch within the vowel. This indicates lack of interest and indecision.

- *"Maybe."*
  With a level inflection, "maybe" conveys a lack of interest.

- *"Okay." "Fine." "Whatever."*
  This can indicate ambivalence.

Practice emphasizing inflections more than you think you need to at first. People often don't inflect words enough for listeners to detect a change, and some audience members may be hard of hearing.

## Enunciation

Public speakers need to articulate each word they speak so that people can understand them. You might slur your speech when you converse naturally – this is very common and most people aren't aware they do it.

# PRACTICE
## PEN EXERCISE

Here's a technique we call the **Pen Exercise**, which is a great way to practice your enunciation. We've included a short clip showing you how to do it in the ★ Present! interactive bundle.

*Involves asking others for feedback.*

### Practice enunciating your words

Try this exercise now, and if you have a talk coming up, practice this for ten to fifteen minutes daily for the best results. Right before you give a presentation, do it for five minutes to warm up your cheek muscles.

- Take a pen and gently bite down on the middle of it.

- Grab a book and start reading out loud. See whether you can understand what you're saying. Articulate as clearly as possible until you can make sense of the words.

- Test yourself by speaking to someone else with the pen in your mouth. Ask whether they can understand what you're saying. If they don't, force yourself to enunciate more and stretch your cheek muscles.

## Speed

It's easier for an audience to follow your talk if you speak slowly. Each of us has a natural speed that lies on a spectrum from slow to fast, and it can be a challenge to change this, so here are some pointers.

- **For slow speakers**
  Note that you will naturally speed up your speaking style when you present. This happens because adrenaline and other stress hormones kick in when you speak in front of an audience.

- **For fast speakers**
  Practice pausing between thoughts and points. Changing your speed is tough at first, so consider giving your audience a heads-up if you're in a setting where people can interact with you during a talk. Take a moment at the start of your presentation to tell your audience that you're a fast speaker and that you're counting on them to raise their hands if you're speaking too quickly.

## Volume and pitch

Whether you're naturally soft-spoken or loud, the audience needs to hear what you're saying.

The best fix? Use a mic.

This is especially important when you have an audience of more than twenty people or are speaking in a room that's bigger than the size of the average living room. A mic can make sure that you're heard and that you don't strain your voice by trying to shout.

A mic can also help speakers in the audience during a Q&A. We recommend that you ask a helper to hand a mic to anyone who wants to ask a question so that both you and the other listeners can hear and understand their question clearly.

Do a mic test before you get onstage and practice using your loudest voice and your quietest voice. If your venue has an A/V team, recruit their help to make sure that the audio sounds great.

If a mic isn't available, you'll need to project your voice so everyone in the audience can hear it. Projecting isn't just speaking loudly, which can tire your voice and make it sound strained. Rather, it's the act of using your diaphragm and breath to speak with strength and clarity – rather than straining, you make your voice bigger. To practice, check out this great Howcast on projecting.[28]

If you have a high-pitched voice, try experimenting with a lower pitch to project your voice when you need to command a room's attention, such as when you're ready to get started with your talk or to bring the focus back to you if you've asked the audience to discuss something with their neighbors during your talk.

Karen learned this trick from her friend, who is a teacher and often needs to get the attention of children at the corners of the playground. She's used it a lot with her son, Ted. She lowers her pitch when she calls upstairs to him with a phrase like, "Hey, Ted, it's dinnertime."

Now it's time to practice these physical and vocal techniques. A quick word of encouragement: changing your speaking style might feel unnatural at first, so if you stick with it and practice regularly, you'll make plenty of progress.

# PRACTICE
## BODY AND VOICE

Practice the physical and verbal style techniques in this chapter. We'll start by focusing on gestures and vocal inflections, and then you can add more techniques once you become comfortable with them.

1. **Set up a video camera for a standing presentation**
   Stand up in front of a video camera so that it captures as much of your body as possible (at least your head and torso). If you're using a laptop to record yourself, put it on a shelf or a stack of books to be closer to your eye level (as opposed to angling the screen upward, which won't be flattering).

2. **Record a two-minute talk about your favorite dessert**
   (Refer to the activity in Chapter 2 if you need a refresher.) As you speak about your dessert, play with gestures and vocal inflections:
   - Use gestures as visual cues. Try signposting, cueing your audience, and mirroring what you're saying.
   - Use vocal inflections to indicate variations in emotion and power.

3. **Watch the video recording**
   Pay attention to your gestures and vocal inflections. How did they affect the delivery of your message?

# PRACTICE CONTINUED

4. **Watch it again to evaluate your overall delivery style**

   This time, pay attention to how you naturally use your body and voice to present, noting any areas where you need improvement:

   - Open body language
   - Eye contact (use your imagination if you're the only person in the room.)
   - Gestures and walking
   - Vocal inflections
   - Enunciation
   - Speed
   - Volume and pitch

5. **Record yourself again**

   Adjust and improve your style for each of the elements above, watch the new video, and take notes. Repeat until you've observed and experimented with all of the techniques.

# RECAP

## CHAPTER 10

### How you deliver a talk is just as important as what you say

Delivery style helps your messages hit home and keeps an audience engaged. There is no one "right" speaking style, so experiment with techniques to find what feels authentic to you.

### Use your body and voice to engage your audience:

- Body language
- Eye contact
- Gestures
- Walking
- Vocal inflections
- Enunciation
- Speed
- Volume and pitch

# 11

# CREATE STUNNING SLIDES

Slides are a final layer on your presentation. They enhance what you're saying with visual appeal, cater to people with visual learning styles, and indicate transitions through different parts of a talk.

You're probably wondering why we've waited until now to talk about building slides. We have three reasons:

1.  We believe that you should be able to develop, practice, and deliver a presentation without slides. Technology can be unpredictable, and we don't want a technical glitch or an organizational mishap to throw you off.

2.  You can lose your creative flow as you hone your story if you jump into making slides too early. Get comfortable creating a strong narrative, and then use slides to complement it.

3.  If you create slides after you've practiced and revised your talk, you'll save time because you won't have to edit your slides as you go along.

Everyone wants to have stunning slides, but they may think they have to be a designer or hire one to create a presentation that's visually appealing. We'll show you how easy it is to do it yourself. Then, we'll share some tips for technical slides and how to make sure your deck shows up on presentation day without a hitch.

## How to create stunning slides

To get started, make sure you're feeling comfortable with your whole talk. It should be fully developed, with a finalized outline that you don't have to rely on when you practice.

Take your outline and turn it into a storyboard. A storyboard is basically like a sequence in a comic. Take out some paper or your computer and create square panels, or "boards." Each one should represent what you're going to be talking about at the time and include ideas for how you might represent the topic visually. Eventually, each board will become a slide. We've included some examples in the ★ Present! interactive bundle.

Next, fire up a slide creator. You can use software like PowerPoint or Keynote (Mac only), and there are also plenty of great web apps that help you create slides and then host them online or download them to your computer. Our favorite is Slidebean.[29]

Turn your boards into slides, adding words and images, and consider what tone you want to convey. Have one idea per slide and minimize visual clutter. Here are three of our tried-and-true slide rules:

1. **Limit the number of words**
   You don't want to be tempted to read from your slides, and you certainly don't want the audience to be reading them either, because it keeps them from connecting with you. Plus, the audience will get bored quickly if all they are doing is reading.

No slide should have more than three to five words on it, unless you are providing bullet points or including quotes. If you are providing bullet points, then there shouldn't be more than five points, and each bullet point shouldn't have more than three to five words on it. And if you are using a longer quote, include an image of the person who said it to ramp up the slide's visual appeal.

Here's an example of a slide where Poornima showcased a quote with the image of the person who said it.

**"We were lucky enough to grow up in an environment where there was always much encouragement to children to pursue intellectual interests; to investigate whatever aroused curiosity."**

**- Orville Wright**

*Figure 11.1*

All text should be aligned the same way: left, right, or center. Pick one style of alignment and have that be the convention for the whole slide deck.

2. **Use images that complement what you're saying**
When you use images, try to make them fill the frame of your slide and make sure they are high resolution. We recommend checking out iStock,[30] Bigstock,[31] or Unsplash[32] for high-quality, royalty-free images.

Here's an example of a slide where Poornima is talking about taking it step-by-step.

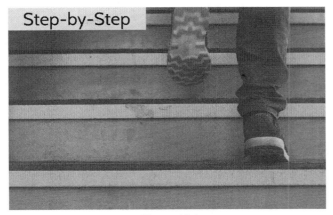

*Figure 11.2*

If you want to include text on an image, then make sure there is enough contrast between the color of the text and the image. Look at the same slide again, noticing contrast.

*Figure 11.3*

3. **Convey tone and emphasis with typography, capitalization, lowercase, and italics (but keep it simple)**
   The visual style of text on slides evokes an emotional response from your audience, just like images do. Your typography sets the tone of your presentation, so choose a

typeface and style that supports the emotion you want your audience to experience. Consider these elements as you style your slides.

- **Typeface**
  A typeface is a set of one or more fonts. We recommend sans serif typefaces for presentations for maximum readability. A clean sans serif font like Helvetica is readable and professional, but it's very common, so you may want to choose another one to make your slides more memorable.

  To show code snippets, we like this recommendation from Scott Hanselman, who writes about giving technical presentations: "Lucida Console, 14 to 18pt, Bold. Consider this my gift to you. This is the most readable, mono-spaced font out there. Courier of any flavor or Arial (or any other proportionally spaced font) is NOT appropriate for code demonstrations, period, full stop."[33]

- **Capitalization**
  Using all caps gives words an urgent tone. Your audience will think they should take notice (or that you're shouting at them). Lowercase typography presents a softer tone.

- **Italics**
  Just like in writing, italics are meant for emphasis. Dr. Brené Brown does a great job of using italics on slides in her TEDx talk on "The Power of Vulnerability."[34]

- **Numbers**
  Numbers can often be used on a slide by themselves to convey the magnitude of a concept.

- **Font size**
  Be sure to use a font size that is visible from the back of a large room. Test this in advance. Guy Kawasaki challenges his readers to use a font no smaller than size thirty on normal slides to force themselves to keep their points salient.[35]

Again, don't forget to keep things simple. When you add emphasis or manipulate your typography, less is more.

*I used to pack my slides with bullets and bullets of information. In hindsight, the slides were my crutch. I relied on them to remind me of every point I wanted to say, every story I wanted to share.*

*But then a friend told me he had made a resolution to eliminate all words from his slides. He had seen someone else give a talk with no text, and it was one of the best talks ever. So except for the title slide, he was going text-free.*

*When my friend first gave it a try, it was like a weight had been removed from his shoulders. Where he used to read from his slides and bore even himself, he found himself talking more conversationally and passionately about the subject. He used to spend hours trying to fit all his text on slides, editing them over and over again to match the words he used during his practice sessions.*

*Now he was free to focus on his stories and messages. He felt more powerful stepping onstage knowing that if he wanted to skip over a point or two, he wouldn't be held hostage by his slides.*

*I decided to give it a try, and it worked. I felt like a weight was lifted from my shoulders as I prepared for and gave the talk. Today, I do my best to limit the words on my slides. While I'm not text-free like my friend, I'm definitely light on it, and I feel more confident with slides now.*

## Tips to finalize your slides

- **Event organizers might have guidelines to comply with**
  Check whether your event organizer will require you to follow a slide template or use certain widescreen resolutions to comply with their projectors.

- **Ensure your presentation software and typeface is available**
  Some event organizers will display the slides for all talks from a single computer to avoid having to swap laptops for each speaker. If this is the case for your event, ask the organizer what presentation software and typefaces will be installed and choose one of those when you create your slides. If you design slides with a typeface that's unavailable on their computer, the software will substitute another one, and you may not be happy with the results.

- **Not all colors show up on projectors**
  If you have doubts, test it in advance. If you are going to be turning off the lights in your room, then you want to make sure that you use a light background. Black or any dark color with white or light text can be hard to read, unless you have an amazing stage and lighting setup, like in Tim Cook's opening of the 2015 WWDC.[36]

- **Make sure data-based visuals make sense at a glance**
  Your audience should be able to understand your graphs and charts in ten to fifteen seconds without explanation.

---

Your data visuals should show trends (like a line or bar graph) or illustrate a clear breakdown (like a pie chart) rather than just display data in a table.

- **Use an appendix for extra information**
  If you have many resources, such as a GitHub link, you can put them in an appendix, which people can review when they get access to your slides after your talk.

- **Make code snippets extra visible**
  To maintain visibility, pare down code snippets to only the most necessary lines – the shorter the better – and try not to go over ten lines. Josh Berkus from PostgreSQL Experts explains in "Give a Great Tech Talk"[37] that when presenting code, you should reformat your examples to use a large, fixed-width font and colors that organize and draw attention to areas the audience should focus on. Break up long lines and zoom in on snippets.

Remember, you can always offer the full information in an appendix slide or on your website – for example, a text file for download, a demo, or a link to your GitHub account. Here's Josh's example of a good way to display code compared with a suboptimal one.

*Figure 11.4*

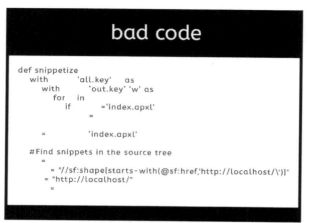

*Figure 11.5*

- **Don't use animated transitions between slides**
  They tend to be distracting, and depending on your computer system or the bandwidth of your connection when presenting a webinar, they may not even show up. Your delivery can provide the dramatic effects instead.

- **Include your contact information**
  On the first and/or last slide of your presentation, include your name and important contact information like your website or your company's website. Also, add the talk name, event name (if applicable), and date. If you plan to release supplements to your talk, like speaker notes or a video of the presentation, you can also include links or information on how to get them. This "metadata" is particularly important if you release the slides online, so people can search for and contextualize your slides.

Follow this activity to create your slides.

---

# PRACTICE

## CREATE STUNNING SLIDES

First, watch Brené Brown's TED talk on "The Power of Vulnerability."[38] As you watch, pay attention to how simple her slides are and how they enhance her narrative.

Next, create a simple and visually compelling slide deck that highlights a clear narrative throughout your talk:

1. Draw a storyboard on paper or on your computer, making a series of boards for the sections you plan to talk about; each board represents a future slide. On each board, jot down ideas for how you might represent points, stories, and examples visually. Pay attention to the overall narrative you're creating. Does it follow your outline evenly?

2. Open a slide creator tool like Slidebean, PowerPoint, or Keynote.

3. Create a title slide with your name and important contact information like your website or your company's website. Add the talk name, event name (if applicable), and date.

# PRACTICE CONTINUED

4. Create one blank slide for each board you sketched out, and then write text for each one (unless it's a visual-only slide, in which case you can just write a note or leave it blank; you'll add visuals in the next step). Limit the number of words on each slide.

5. Once you've finished creating text-only slides, go back and add images that complement text.

6. Go through the slide deck again and style text with typography, capitalization, lowercase, and italics.

7. If you've presented data or code, double-check whether an audience member can scan it quickly and understand the point you're trying to make without explanation.

8. Create an appendix if you need one to give your audience additional resources. Add your name, contact information, the name of the talk, the date, and the event name, if applicable.

# RECAP

## CHAPTER 11

**Create your slides after your talk is developed and you've practiced**

You should be able to deliver a presentation without slides. When you jump into creating slides before your content is finished, you can lose focus on your key messages and stories, and you will waste time if you need to change your presentation after your slides are finished.

**We have three rules for designing simple and stunning slides:**

1. Limit the number of words on each slide.

2. Use images that complement what you are saying.

3. Play with typography, capitalization, lowercase, and italics to convey emotions.

# PART IV

## THE FINISHING TOUCHES

You've experimented with delivery styles using your body and voice and learned how to accompany your talk with slides. As your presentation day approaches, there are a few things to prepare to make sure it goes off without a hitch.

First, get ready for audience interaction like Q&A sessions and hecklers (if you can call hecklers audience interaction). Learning a few pro strategies to handle questions and mishaps on the fly will make you feel more confident going into your talk and will impress your audience as you steer the conversation. We cover these in Chapters 12 and 13.

Chapter 14 has checklists to help you prepare logistics for the day of your presentation, as well as what to do when you arrive at the venue to get in the best mindset to present.

You've done all this amazing work, so you might as well promote your talk so more people know about it, right? We actually think that promoting your talk online is a must, both before and after it happens. In Chapter 15, we'll show you how to use the web to increase your talk's reach and raise your profile as a public speaker and expert on your topic.

And then? It's game time.

# 12
## FINESSE Q&A SESSIONS

Many talks have an official Q&A session once the main presentation ends, where audience members can ask the speaker questions. Plenty of talks don't have designated Q&A time, but people may still ask the speaker questions by raising their hand during the session or in private afterward.

Anticipating a Q&A session is nerve-racking for some people. Most of our students tell us they are worried about being asked a question they can't answer, and that this is the root cause of their stage fright. It holds them back from giving talks.

Do you feel the same way? Do you want your Q&A session to be as polished and powerful as your main presentation? Well, we have a few surefire strategies to help you out.

With a little preparation and some techniques in your tool belt to use on the fly, you'll be able to host helpful, intimate Q&A sessions that add depth to your talks - even if you don't have all the answers.

## How to be a great Q&A host

You're behind the steering wheel. It's your responsibility to facilitate Q&A sessions so that it's helpful for all audience members, whether they want to ask a question or would rather just listen.

When you receive a question, always do these three things before giving your answer:

- **Thank the person who asked the question**
  Give them a simple "Thanks for asking that question!" or "Thanks for asking the first question!" You want to applaud them because for many people, it is scary to get up and ask something. This helps them relax and actually listen to your response rather than feel self-conscious about whether the question is a silly one. It also encourages other audience members to ask questions next.

- **Repeat the question**
  Yes, every time, even if the person asking the question has a mic. This does two things:

  - You confirm for yourself what the question is. Sometimes the person asking the question will hear your restatement and realize that they didn't convey it properly.

  - You make sure the audience understands the question, because even if the question is heard, sometimes it goes by so quickly that listeners won't catch it the first time around.

- **Pause before answering a question**
  It's okay to take a time-out. You don't have to respond immediately. This has two effects:

- It shows that you're being thoughtful and not just regurgitating some canned response.

- It gives you time to think and gives the audience a little mental break.

These three techniques will make you look professional, help you avoid misunderstandings, and ensure that everyone in the room has a chance to hear the question and benefit from your answer.

There may be times when the audience doesn't have any questions, or they're all shy and no one's eager to ask the first one. In this case, you can always turn things around and ask them a question. To make this work, choose one with some parameters or specificity, because questions that are too open ended can feel daunting. For example, you could ask, "What is the one thing you learned from my talk?" or "In the last session, someone asked about the best resources for learning about growth hacking. What do you think?"

On the flip side, your audience members may be too generous with their words. If someone takes more than thirty seconds (one minute at the very most) to ask their question, kindly interrupt them. Here are two examples of how to do this. If they take a long time to get to their question or spend excess time clarifying it, say, "I hear your question. Let me take a stab at answering it." If they disguise a complicated comment as an inquiry, try, "So ... I appreciate you standing up to comment. Do you have a question?"

If you get a two-part question, repeat both questions for the audience, then answer the first one before you go on to the next, with a clear transition between the two.

## How to limit the surprise factor

Decrease the chances of getting a question that catches you off guard. With some pre-talk homework, you can often predict what people will ask about and have an answer prepared.

We touched on this in Chapters 3 and 4 when you created a topic teaser and then focused it for a specific ideal audience. Going back to that technique, specifically the section on audience questions, brainstorm about what kind of help the audience needs most as it relates to your subject.

- **Audience questions**
  Anticipate the audience's needs. What are the most common questions you can think of? Do you have resources that you want to point people to? Are there any shortcuts they should know about or be wary of? What do you wish you had known before you worked on this project?

You can also use friends and colleagues to help you anticipate questions. Ask them to brainstorm about the questions above. Or take a less direct approach: when you discuss your topic with them or practice your talk, notice which clarifying questions they ask and write them down. You can even ask them to jot down questions that surface in their minds as they hear you speak.

Another powerful technique for minimizing surprises is the **Mind Reader Strategy.**

When people come into the room for your talk, you can approach them and ask them what one or two things they're hoping to get out of the presentation. Write them down and review them for a few minutes before starting your talk.

This has several interesting benefits. Just like the pre-talk prep home-work, it lessens the chance that you'll be blindsided by questions because you've already gotten a sneak peek of what the audience cares about. Their Q&A questions will often stem from these topics.

This strategy also gives you a sense of whether your talk itself is on target. If you're concerned that your talk is too long or short, you can focus it on the things your audience members say they care about (we recommend this on-the-fly presentation adjustment for presenters who are a bit more experienced with public speaking).

Your goal is to give the audience the impression that you've read their mind and covered exactly what they wanted to hear.

You may not be able to cover everything the audience cares about in full during your presentation, so consider opening up your Q&A with a question directed at the audience that touches on one of these topics. This lets you borrow some time from the Q&A session to make sure you're meeting the audience's needs, and it also takes the pressure off the audience to come up with the very first question of the session.

The Mind Reader Strategy has a funny way of giving your event an aura of goodwill. It shows people you care about them as soon as they walk into the room, and it engages them early on, lowering the chance that they'll become a "tough audience" (more on this in the next chapter).

## Two techniques to handle challenging questions

Here are two of our favorite techniques to use when audience members ask us questions we don't know or ones we can't answer with a simple response.

- **Crowdsource Strategy**

  When you get a question that stumps you, it's perfectly reasonable to say, "I don't know." But don't stop there. Your goal is to help the person asking the question resolve their query at one point or another.

  Recruit the help of the audience with the **Crowdsource Strategy**: "Can anyone in the audience answer this question?" More often than not, someone will shout out a response. The added benefit is that you end up engaging the other audience members.

- **Take It Offline Strategy**

  You don't want a complicated question to take over your entire Q&A session. If you think a question will take you a long time to answer, or that the person who asked it will have many follow-ups, try the **Take It Offline Strategy**.

  Say, "That's a great question, and I want to make sure I address it adequately. Come talk to me right after the Q&A and I'll be happy to go into more depth. And if anyone else wants to listen, they can come, too." Or, encourage people to get in touch with you by email if they want to learn more.

  You can also point toward outside resources that might answer the question, or you can offer to investigate the issue separately and stay in touch.

If you practice the techniques here, you'll gain the confidence you need to stride onstage and field questions, whatever they may be.

# RECAP

## CHAPTER 12

### Your job during Q&A is to guide the conversation

- Keeps the dialog flowing by brainstorming questions in advance, and use the **Mind Reader Strategy** to reduce the chance of being blindsided by a question.

- The **Crowdsource Strategy** helps you answer questions that stump you.

- The **Take It Offline Strategy** prevents a complicated question from taking over your session.

### Before answering a question, do three things:

- Thank the person who asked the question.

- Restate the question.

- Take a quiet pause before answering.

# 13

# HANDLE HECKLERS AND TOUGH AUDIENCES

L et's say you're presenting and can't help but notice people chatting in the fifth row. What do you do?

And what if the fire alarm in the building goes off? Or what if you get a heckler who blurts things out at you from the audience?

No matter how much you prepare, your talk is subject to forces of nature and chance. You're human, your audience is human, and you're presenting in the real world, where mishaps and interruptions just happen. These are not your fault.

But you can learn how to deal with them smoothly to give your audience the best experience possible. Here are a few common issues that can come up during presentations.

## Tough crowds

Tough crowds can happen to anyone, and there are many reasons why your audience might be unresponsive during your talk. It has nothing to do with the quality of your delivery. They might be a little bit tired because your talk is happening right before or after lunch. Maybe they're just a quiet bunch or have already watched hours of presentations.

You might be able to spot this early on. If you're giving a long talk, more than twenty minutes, then take the time before you start your presentation to get them to move. Something as simple as, "Show of hands: How many of you have an app in the App Store?" Or you could say, "Those of you who run a social media account for your company, please stand up."

You can also interject these questions in the middle of your talk if you feel the audience might be bored or distracted.

And if you do happen to present right before lunch, tell the audience, "I know it's right before lunch, and you're probably all hungry, so don't worry, I will get you guys out a little bit early so you're the first in line." Then do your best to end a little bit early by cutting down on Q&A time and telling people that you'll stick around if they have additional questions.

## Overactive audiences

Sometimes your room is the opposite of sleepy – it might have a ton of activity, such as people entering and exiting the room a lot. Don't let this throw you off. Remind yourself that activity is often unavoidable, and sometimes people just have to go to the bathroom, take an important call, or tend to a commitment.

Even if the members of your audience start leaving in droves, keep going. It often has nothing to do with you, and throwing in the towel is unnecessary. Poornima once had an audience where nearly everyone left except for a handful of people. She was worried, so she asked around afterward to figure out why. Turns out they all had a pre-scheduled team meeting during her talk, except for the five who stayed.

If a couple of people are trying to talk to one another quietly during your presentation in a way that distracts you or your audience, intervene politely: "Hi, my friends in the second row, do you have a question?"

Overactive audiences can be unnerving, but remember: it's probably not because of the quality of your work.

## An audience too small for the room

If you're speaking in a large room and your audience is on the small side, people will naturally spread out. This makes it difficult to engage them and weakens the energy of the room.

So before you get started, say something like, "Since there are just a few of you, let's get cozy and make this more interactive. Come on up to the first and second row. I promise I won't bite."

Don't ask them to move. Tell them to, and they will.

A small audience can work in your favor. If you bring them together in the front of the room for an intimate session, they'll be more engaged and participatory than if they were in a larger group. They will feel like they got extra value out of your talk as part of a small group that got special attention. They'll tell their friends and coworkers afterward, "Oh, you missed out!"

Recently, we taught a workshop that was supposed to include fifty people, but only five were able to show up. We had them sit in the front row for about four hours, and they loved it.

## Emergencies

Sometimes unexpected issues just happen. As the speaker, remember that you're the steward of your audience's good experience, and they'll look to you for cues on how to interpret an issue and behave in response.

---

If a fire alarm goes off, just roll with it and encourage everyone to exit the building. Yes, this has happened to us before – at the start of a daylong workshop, no less. When we returned to the classroom, we simply summarized what we had already covered and proceeded with the rest of our presentation.

It's rare, but you might need to get an important message to an audience member and don't want to draw attention to them. A tactful way to handle this is to create a short distraction for the rest of the audience members.

Karen remembers sitting in the audience of a talk when there was an announcement that the police had found a dog in a parked car, and they were going to break the window in five minutes. Then the organizer read the license plate number. Can you imagine how embarrassed you'd be if you were the person who had to get up and go tend to your dog? The speaker anticipated this and encouraged everyone to stand up and stretch, which allowed the person to leave without being shamed.

## Technical issues

If there's a technical issue with your mic or slides, let the audience know how you are going to handle it. For example, "It looks like the projection equipment is on the fritz. Let's give the A/V team one minute to address the problem. If they can't figure it out, I'll give the talk without my slides."

Then, do something to keep the audience engaged. Ask them anything. Where did they travel from? How did they hear about the talk? You want to fill the time while someone is sorting out the technical issue. If you need to be involved in fixing it, tell the audience to stand and stretch, and reiterate that if it's not fixed after one minute then you'll proceed. This prevents them from getting too distracted. And remember, to prevent these issues, test technical equipment a few days in advance or show up early on the day of the presentation.

If you end up without a mic or slides, you will be fine (because you've practiced enough without them!) and your audience will understand the circumstances.

## Hecklers

Ah, hecklers. Public speakers have different reactions to them. Some fear them, some despise them, and some just accept that they can happen to anyone.

We want you to be part of the third camp, and to always remember that heckling is not your fault. You might think it's a sign that you're giving a bad talk, but it rarely is, and even if you are having an off day or make a small slipup, that is no grounds for someone to be disrespectful.

We use two techniques to handle hecklers. The first is called the **Bouncer Technique.**

Here's how it works at a large conference. Conferences often assign speakers a "handler" - someone who guides you before and after your talk. Handlers also keep a close eye on the audience. If someone acts up, the handler approaches them like a bouncer at a club and kindly disposes of them.

In this scenario, you don't have to lift a finger. All you have to do is act natural and keep the rest of the audience engaged with your talk. It sounds strange, but it's the most professional way to get through the issue.

A couple of years ago, when Poornima was speaking in Canada, someone started catcalling her during her talk. Turns out he had gotten a little tipsy at the bar. Within thirty seconds, two people approached the heckler and escorted him out of the room. Poornima just kept speaking, and no one thought anything of the incident.

If you're attending a smaller event or one that just doesn't have a lot of staff, you could ask a friend in the audience or someone in charge to intervene if anyone starts to heckle. They can ask the offender to "follow them" out of the room.

Or, you might need to take matters into your own hands with the **Three Strikes You're Out Strategy.**

- **Strike 1**
  When you first hear a heckler, acknowledge them immediately, but give them the benefit of the doubt. Say something like, "Hi, my friend in the second row, with the blue shirt on, do you have a comment or a question?"

  It's important that you be specific about the location (second row), and use descriptions that aren't offensive (blue shirt). We might mistake people for hecklers when they are just asking a question, are hard of hearing, or have a chronic medical condition, which is why we want to show compassion first. If their answer is polite, then respond and move on.

- **Strike 2**
  If they continue to interject inappropriately, then call them out again. Say, "Thank you, I'll be happy to chat with you after the talk."

- **Strike 3**
  If they persist, then this is when you have to do the Bouncer Technique yourself. But you'll have to stick with

---

using your words. We do not recommend approaching them physically.

You can use the audience as a shield by saying something like, "I apologize, I'm trying to do my best to share my presentation and get everyone out on time, but I cannot do that with any more interruptions. So, my friend in the second row, with the blue shirt on, I'm going to have to kindly ask you to stop interjecting. If that's not possible, then I'll have to ask you to leave."

By this point, someone in the audience might help you out. If not, then excuse yourself and leave the room to get an event organizer to help you out.

We realize that you might not like confrontation, but you should address the heckler and resolve the issue as soon as possible because it can upset or distract the audience. And once you do, you'll be back on track to have a great presentation.

# RECAP

## CHAPTER 13

### You can't control everything about presentation day

Mishaps, emergencies, interruptions, and technical issues happen to the best of us. Don't let them ruffle you; try to guide the audience through these issues gracefully so they have a good experience under the circumstances.

### Getting heckled is rare, but it can happen

Use these two techniques to handle hecklers on the spot:

- Bouncer Technique
- Three Strikes You're Out Strategy

# 14

## PREP FOR PRESENTATION DAY

Before the day of your talk, prepare a few details to make sure everything goes smoothly. We'll be rooting for you!

### Visit the room in advance

If you've never been to the venue at which you'll present, ask the event organizer whether you can practice in your presentation room a few days before the event. We recommend this for everyone, especially those with stage fright. You'll get the chance to practice walking around on the stage (or decide where to stand, if there isn't a stage), to predict whether you'll be able to see people in the back of the audience, and to iron out technical kinks if you plan to use slides or microphones.

Whether or not you can practice there, visiting the room in advance is a good idea to mentally prepare and make sure you don't get lost.

### Plan your presentation-day schedule

Knowing your plan can make you feel more calm as the day approaches, and it prevents mishaps.

- Make sure you know how to get to the venue and what transportation method you'll use.

- Decide what time you need to arrive in order to set up and still have time to mingle with the audience.

- Think about how early you need to leave home. Add a buffer for traffic.

- Consider whether you'll have time to network with people when you finish your talk, or whether you'll have to run off to a work meeting or another talk instead.

## Back up slides and other electronic assets

If you have slides or a video, upload a copy to the cloud or a memory stick in case there is a problem with the laptop that will project them. For slides, also upload a PDF version so you can display them without having the software you used to create them. (If, for example, you need to project using the organizer's laptop instead of your own, the software might not be available and you'll have problems when loading slides.)

Being a little paranoid can pay off. Karen remembers arriving to give a talk and finding she couldn't get her laptop to connect to the room projector. The host quickly procured a working laptop, and Karen downloaded the PDF version she had stored in the cloud the night before.

## Have a pre-presentation routine

When presentation day arrives, have a plan for what you'll do right before the talk. For example, here's what you might do if you arrive one hour before you're set to go onstage:

- Set down your belongings, keeping a watch, phone, or clock in sight so you can keep track of time leading up to your presentation and while you speak.

- Set up your slides or microphone if needed.

- If appropriate, prepare business cards so you're ready to hand them out after your talk and take off your conference badge or name tag if you're wearing one. (We prefer not wearing the name tag while we present because it creates visual clutter.)

- Find a quiet spot backstage or in a restroom to practice the stage fright busters we teach in Chapter 9, like striking a power pose.

- Warm up your articulation muscles with the Pen Exercise from Chapter 10.

- Mingle with the audience. This helps you make friends, helps you reduce stage fright, and gives you an opportunity to use the Mind Reader Strategy from Chapter 12, in which you ask people what they're hoping to learn from the talk to see whether you need to cover anything extra during Q&A.

- Have fun and take the pressure off: your goal is confidence and connection with the audience, not perfection.

# RECAP

## CHAPTER 14

**Get ready for presentation day:**

- Visit the presentation room and practice there (if possible).

- Prepare your schedule in advance to ensure you arrive on time.

- Back up slides and other assets like videos.

- Think through the last-minute preparations you need to do between the time you arrive at the venue and the time when you step onstage.

**When it's time to give your talk, have fun!**

# 15

## PROMOTE YOUR TALK

If you've done a lot of work to create a presentation, you might as well get as many people to see it as possible by promoting it online – both before and after you give it.

We'll show you how to use the web (social media, your own website, LinkedIn, etc.) to promote an upcoming talk. We'll also show you how to share the collateral of a talk you've already given, like slides or a video recording, so that it's available to your audience after the talk is over – and to reach more people.

Feel shy or uncomfortable promoting your presentations? Keep in mind these benefits:

- Promoting your talk before it happens can cause a higher event turnout.

- People will be more aware of your speaking activity, whether or not they attend your talk. This strengthens your reputation as a thought leader on your topic and can lead to more speaking opportunities.

- Publishing your content on the web once the talk is over extends its life, reaching people who couldn't come to your event, including people around the world whom you may never cross paths with otherwise.

Let's get started with a few promotional techniques to do leading up to your talk.

## Promote your talk online before you present

Before your talk, create a short teaser post about the event and publish it on social media about a week or two beforehand so more people in your network will attend or spread the word. If you only have a few days, that's fine – better late than never.

Write a one-sentence summary of the talk's focus, list the types of takeaways you'll be giving, and add the time, date, and location. Include a link for people to find out more and register for the event, if applicable. Here's an example of a post Poornima put on her blog before her speaking gig at Deploy 2010.[39]

> *I will be speaking at Deploy 2010, hosted by Seattle 2.0 on Thursday, June 24, at Bell Harbor Conference Center in Seattle, WA. The focus of my talk is pre-launch planning for startups, geared toward engineering. I aim to cover technologies to use, best practices, and trade-offs to make before crunch time!*

Post the blurb wherever you can. Use LinkedIn, Facebook, Twitter, and other social media sites, and turn it into an article if you have a blog. You can also send it to your company's internal mailing list. If you are attending a big conference or event, have the organizers post it on the event's blog and social network pages to spread the word.

Before you give a presentation, make sure to complete the following activity. It might feel uncomfortable to promote your talk, but it will help you reach more people and raise your professional profile within your network.

# PRACTICE
## WRITE A PROMO FOR YOUR UPCOMING TALK

Write a short teaser post to promote your presentation online. Jot down a few sentences about your talk (five at the most). Include the following information:

- The name of the event you'll be speaking at and a link, if applicable
- The time, date, and location
- A one-sentence summary of your talk and its purpose
- A few types of takeaways the audience can expect

Post it online on multiple platforms:

- LinkedIn
- Twitter
- Facebook
- Your website or blog
- Your company's internal forum or mailing list
- The blog or mailing list of the event you're presenting at, if applicable

## Promote your talk online after you present

When you finish giving a presentation, treat yourself to a nice beer or root beer float to celebrate. Then get back to work. There's plenty of mileage left in the talk you just gave.

Promoting your talk online after it's over has many benefits. These are just a few of them:

- People who attended will be able to review your talk, reach out, and share your work with others to spread the word about what you do.

- It's a great conversation starter. Just because someone – whether it's a colleague or a stranger – couldn't make it to your presentation doesn't mean they aren't interested in what you had to say. They may want to connect, and this can lead to opportunities.

- People around the world whom you normally would never cross paths with will be able to see your presentation and benefit from your work.

- You'll get more invitations to speak. There may be other event organizers who are interested in your topic, and if they see your work online, they'll know you're a subject matter expert and reach out to you. Sometimes this can result in an easy copy-and-paste of your talk, saving you tons of prep time. Just because you've given a talk once to a particular audience doesn't mean you can't give it again to another.

  Poornima once gave a talk in Europe, and then an event organizer reached out to her to ask if she would be open to giving it again in San Francisco. It was a great way to amplify her message without putting in much extra time.

If you feel uncomfortable promoting your presentation, remember that it's not a selfish act; you're sharing your expertise and knowledge to help others learn and benefit. There are two things for you to prepare: presentation assets and a recap post.

## Put together shareable assets from your presentation

We encourage you to share as many assets from your presentation as possible. If you want to spread your ideas, don't keep them where no one can see them.

First, you can share a recording of your talk if you or the event organizer arranged a video or audio recording. The recording may come in the form of a video or audio file attachment, or you can upload it to a service like YouTube or Vimeo.

Next, share your slides. One way to package them is in a PDF; you can send this PDF attachment to the event organizer and have them email it to the attendees, for example. And for more reach, you can post them on SlideShare,[40] which takes just a couple of minutes. SlideShare hosts your slides online, gives you a specific URL you can share with people, and makes your presentation discoverable to people browsing SlideShare.net or searching Google for slides on your topic. You may be surprised at how many people will view them.

When you upload your slide deck, be sure to tag it with some keywords related to your topic, which will make it more discoverable. You can also link your SlideShare account to your LinkedIn profile or embed the SlideShare presentation on your personal website, if you have one.

You can also create an annotated slide deck, which shows the text from your talk next to its accompanying slide. Many people enjoy reading annotated slide decks, and they're not that much work to create. You can do this by saving each of your slides as a picture and pasting some notes or an excerpt of the transcript from your talk next to each slide. You can publish your annotated slide deck as a PDF, a SlideShare, or a blog post.

Here are two examples of annotated slides Karen created after her talks: "Turning Risk into Opportunity"[41] and "Measure Impact, Not Activity."[42]

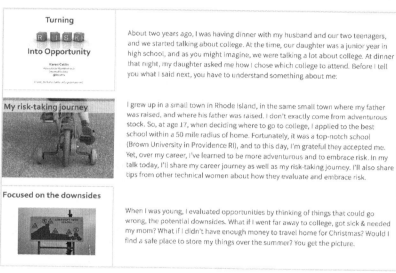

*Figure 11.6*

Note that we don't usually release slides before a presentation because we want to create a little anticipation in the audience for our talks. During our talks, we'll often let the audience know that we will make the slides available online and send them out after the presentation.

## Tie it all together with a recap post

Once you have your presentation assets in order, you can package them into a recap post that you publish online to give people a glimpse of what your talk was about. You can write a recap post

---

Present! A Techie's Guide to Public Speaking

without assets, but including some slides or a recording lets people dig deeper if they find your written post interesting and want more information.

If you're thinking, "I'm not a writer," no problem. Your post can be short, and you can reuse the proposal you wrote for your talk and tweak it a bit so it's in past tense. Make sure to include the location where you gave the talk, why you were invited to speak, quick highlights of what you covered, and links to assets. If you like, you can include common questions people brought up.

If you like to write, you can create a longer post about the topic of your talk that presents your viewpoints, takeaways, supporting arguments, and stories. Use your notes or original outline to write a rough overview of what you said while it's still fresh in your mind. Turn these notes into an article or an annotated slide deck (as described above).

You can publish the article on your personal blog or company blog. If you don't have a blog, you can easily host it on LinkedIn's Publishing Platform,[43] where it will be affiliated with your LinkedIn account, or Medium,[44] an easy-to-use blog publishing platform. Then share the link to your post on your favorite social media channels, such as LinkedIn, Facebook, or Twitter. It's okay to post on more than one network. You might feel like you are bombarding people, but most people have an affinity to particular networks and don't check the others, so they might only catch your post on one or maybe two of them.

By keeping your presentation alive on the web, you're helping more people over a longer period of time.

# RECAP

## CHAPTER 15

### Before your talk, promote it online

Write a post to promote your talk on social media in advance, using LinkedIn, Twitter, Facebook, and the event organizer's accounts if applicable. This improves turnout and lets your network know that you're an active public speaker in your domain.

### After your talk, publish a recap and presentation assets

Write a recap post of your talk and distribute presentation assets. This helps your audience learn more and lets you reach people who didn't attend your presentation. Include:

- Video recordings
- Audio recordings
- Slides
- Talk notes, transcripts, or annotated slides

# PART V
## SPECIAL TALK FORMATS

Here are some extra tips for a few presentation formats that are common in the tech world. If you're creating one of these talks, we recommend reading through the chapter and then revisiting Part II to find a topic, develop the presentation, and practice it.

Chapter 16 covers lightning talks - a short and sweet way to present an idea and get your name out there. They are also a great way to try speaking at a public event for the first time. Chapter 17, on the other hand, shows you how to dive deeper into your topic during a longer time slot of thirty minutes or even more than sixty minutes.

Panels let you do public speaking in a collective group. You can moderate a panel or participate as a panelist. It's fun! Chapter 18 gives you tips on how to be a great panel host and guest.

If you want to give your talk on the web or distribute it online for wider reach, consider creating a webinar or podcast. In Chapter 19, we'll give you tips on how to optimize your talk for these formats. We won't be covering how to do product pitches or software demos.

For specific guidance on these special formats, we recommend you read Great Demo!: How to Create and Execute Stunning Software Demonstrations[45] and Pitch Anything: An Innovative Method for Presenting, Persuading, and Winning the Deal.[46]

# 16
## LIGHTNING TALKS

A lightning talk is a short presentation on a topic, usually no longer than five minutes.

Lightning talks let you get a message out there with considerably less preparation and time commitment than a typical talk. And if you're new to public speaking, they're a great way to get your feet wet, especially if you don't have enough content to fill a long time slot or you're worried about keeping an audience engaged for an extended period of time.

Some conferences will have an entire session of lightning talks in which speakers get up and present back to back. This format gives the audience a chance to learn from a broad range of topics while holding their attention in short spurts.

Here we'll share how to structure a typical lightning talk. There are other styles out there, and we'll leave it up to you to discover more about them. For example, an Ignite[47] talk requires a presenter to speak with twenty slides that auto-advance every fifteen seconds over five minutes. PechaKucha,[48] which is quite popular in Japan, is similar to Ignite in that it uses twenty auto-advancing slides for twenty seconds for a total of six minutes and forty seconds.

## The benefits of lightning talks

Lightning talks are generally five minutes long and focus on one or two main takeaways. We like them for several reasons:

- **They're quick**
  You're only on for a short time, which means your talk is over before you have time to worry about what to say next.

- **They're faster to prepare**
  There's less material to prep than in a typical talk.

- **You're forced to be concise**
  You don't have to worry about providing lots of in-depth material. Instead, you can focus on one or two takeaways.

- **You still get visibility**
  Lightning talks give you credibility and can create follow-on opportunities. Because they are short and you'll be limited in how much ground you can cover, it's likely that audience members will come up to you afterward and ask questions. You'll meet new people and have some great discussions.

- **They're perfect for keeping an audience's attention**
  You don't need to worry about people walking out halfway through your talk or about how to reignite their attention every twenty minutes.

If you're a more experienced speaker, you may want to have a lightning version of every longer talk you create. Events you'd like to speak at may not have many long spots available, and the event organizers might be looking for people who can fill in short blocks of time. In general, you can use this short version of your talk to get your name out, introduce people to your work, and convince audience members to see one of your longer talks, either at the same event, at another conference, or online.

## How to structure a lightning talk

Since you only have about five minutes, every minute counts. You have to keep things brief and to the point. Choose one or two salient takeaways to focus on in your lightning talk.

When you deliver a lightning talk, you can follow this flow:

- Deliver your introduction.
- Preview the takeaways you'll cover.
- Explain each one in order.
- Deliver your conclusion.
- End with a call-to-action
  (a Final Ask, which we explain below).

Let's talk about how long you should spend on each of these sections, starting with the introduction.

We recommend that you review the story you created in Chapter 5 and use it to kick off your talk. Remove all details that don't relate to your talk's takeaways. You'll want to compress your story down to about sixty seconds and no more than ninety seconds if you plan to share it all during the introduction. Alternately, you can reveal your story's context and problem in the introduction, and then use the Slow Reveal Technique to layer in the rest of your story throughout your presentation so that you can get to the takeaways sooner.

If your original proposal relies on multiple stories, we recommend that you choose just one story to highlight the points in your lightning talk. If you try to add multiple analogies or stories to a short talk, it can be hard for the audience to keep track of what's going on.

After the introduction, you'll provide a little motivation for the audience to continue listening by briefly previewing the takeaways you'll cover in your talk, essentially highlighting how they'll benefit from it.

Then, discuss your takeaways and supporting points. This is the real meat of the talk, so we recommend spending about ninety seconds on each takeaway (you can take a little longer if you only have one).

Finally, allocate about thirty to sixty seconds for the conclusion of your talk, where you'll review the points quickly. We recommend that you refer back to your original story and restate its theme to tie everything together. Include a final call-to-action (more on this in the next section).

Does a talk like this seem like it lacks substance? If you answer "yes," you're right to feel that way. Lightning talks don't go deep because they're meant to whet people's appetites to learn even more from you later.

## The Final Ask

This brings us to the very last part of your lightning talk: the call-to-action. Any talk can have a call-to-action, but it's a key part of a lightning talk precisely because they are so light on information. You need to tell your audience how to find more of your work and contact you after your talk. This is a way to plug your work and show-case opportunities to connect with you. We call it the **Final Ask**.

Last year, Poornima gave several lightning talks when she published her first book, *How to Transform Your Ideas into Software Products*. Each talk covered only one or two topics, so they were quite light. In the conclusion, she said, "If you want to learn more, then check out my book. I'll be signing copies after this talk."

People were genuinely interested to learn more when they heard Poornima's plug because her talk piqued their curiosity. No one came up to her and said, "Ugh, I can't believe you promoted your book!" They just said, "Great talk, and I'd love to learn more!" or "Kudos to you for self-publishing; that must have been a lot of work!"

Adding a call-to-action might feel like you're sneaking in a commercial, but don't worry. You're not creating an obligation for anyone in the audience. You're creating an opportunity.

To improve the odds that people will heed your call-to-action, consider creating a short handout, displaying a promotional sign, or setting out your business cards for them to pick up.

When Karen gave a lightning talk on the Male Allies project, she showcased a bingo card the project had created (it was full of examples of how to be better allies for women in the tech industry). Her call-to-action? To bring the bingo card back to their offices to generate discussions about gender diversity. As you can guess, she had copies of the Male Allies bingo card for the audience to pick up after her talk. It also had the URL for the project, www.maleallies.com,[49] printed along the bottom for anyone who wanted more information.

## What about Q&A?

Often an event will feature a series of lightning talks in a row, and to keep things moving along, the organizers may not hold Q&A

after each talk. At most, they might allocate just a couple of minutes or ask a preselected question.

So, to get the most out of your lightning talk, hang around afterward. People will find you and ask their questions then.

## Keep the focus on you, not on visuals

Proceed with caution with slides for a lightning talk. It can be difficult for you to keep pace and for the audience to follow.

Some people use decks for lightning talks, but we usually avoid it. If you choose to go the safe route, just make one title slide with visually appealing imagery and your contact information. You can also limit yourself to one slide per minute (roughly five slides for the whole presentation).

What about demos and videos? We've seen presenters try to do a demo or show a video during their lightning talks. We recommend that you don't do this for two reasons:

- There just isn't enough time, and if you experience a technical delay or glitch, it will cut into the rest of your talk. Instead, in the conclusion, let the audience know how they can see a demo or watch a video. That can serve as your Final Ask.

- It takes time away from engaging with you. Five to seven minutes is a pretty short time period for you to establish credibility and engage with an audience. If you spend that time directing your audience's attention away, then people don't really get a chance to connect with you because they're focused on your video, slides, or physical demo.

We also caution against showing code snippets if you're giving a technical lightning talk. It can take people time to read through them, and they'll miss what you're saying in the meantime. Instead, share a description of the major problem you experienced, your solution, and the results. If they want to dig into the details, they can speak with you afterward, or you can point them to resources like tutorials and your source code repository.

## Sample lightning talks

Ready to learn by example? Watch these lightning talks. You'll see that they are brief but quickly capture the audience's attention, get to the theme of the talk, and provide reasons why the topic is important so that the audience wants to learn more.

Our first favorite example of a lightning talk is "404, the Story of a Page Not Found," by Renny Gleeson.[50] We'd like you to notice a few things about his presentation. He opens by saying that he wants to tell a quick story about a 404 page and a lesson that was learned as a result. He quickly defines the term to bring everyone in the room up to speed: "To start, it probably helps to have an understanding of what a 404 page actually is."

He then introduces the problem with most 404 pages and explains why the audience should care. He also weaves in the story of how a startup in Renny's incubator, Athletepath, added a funny video to their 404 page and how other companies followed suit. His talk then reveals its main takeaway: even an error page can be an opportunity to show a brand's personality and make a connection with their users.

Another great example is Margaret Gould Stewart's talk "How YouTube Thinks about Copyright."[51] While this is generally a broad topic, you'll notice that Margaret does a great job of narrowing the scope. Pay attention to how she relates the copyright topic to the audience from the very beginning to get their attention. She explains the issue and illustrates YouTube's copyrighted material detection solution with one example: a Chris Brown music video. Margaret then explains the magnitude of the solution and concludes with a takeaway around the benefits of having a flexible rights management system.

Chris Morris gives an entertaining lightning talk at RailsConf 2013 on "Technical Intimidation."[52] He opens the talk with funny, real-life examples of pressure to know everything about Ruby on Rails, and then settles on his main message: software is hard. Chris's talk is an example of one that uses many slides to illustrate his points. Watch it to get a sense for how this influences the presentation. Note that his main message, "Software is hard," gets its own slide and the biggest font size in the entire deck. He also includes contact information at the end and links to supplementary information, like his blog post about the same topic, in the YouTube video description.

A final note: these speakers all paced themselves despite the short time slot. Fast talkers, be wary. A lightning talk isn't an excuse to speed up. You still want to maintain a pace that your audience can comprehend, so keep it slow and allocate time for pauses.

# PRACTICE
## CREATE A LIGHTNING TALK

Create an outline for your lightning talk, using your proposal from Chapter 6 if you completed it.

Jot down the following elements:

1. **Introduction**
   Start with a story or another opener.

2. **Preview**
   Motivate the audience to keep listening and list the one to two takeaways you'll cover.

3. **Takeaways**
   Spend sixty to ninety seconds on each takeaway.

4. **Conclusion**
   Refer back to the original story and quickly recap the takeaways.

5. **Call-to-action**
   Close with a call-to-action or Final Ask to tell the audience how they can engage with your work after the talk.

# PRACTICE CONTINUED

Once you have an outline, work through Chapter 7 to flesh out the content of your lightning talk and practice it.

Recording yourself is particularly useful for lightning talks because time is a big concern. Pay attention to whether your time is spread out evenly among sections, and make sure your introduction is only sixty to ninety seconds long. If you tell a story at the start of your talk, consider using the Slow Reveal Technique to distribute it throughout instead.

# RECAP

## CHAPTER 16

**A lightning talk is short and sweet (usually five minutes long)**

The purpose of a lightning talk is to give the audience a taste of your work. Focus on one or two takeaways, then promote your projects with a Final Ask at the end of your talk so they can learn more from you if they're interested.

**The structure of a lightning talk:**

1. Introduction
2. Preview of takeaways
3. Explanation of takeaways
4. Conclusion
5. Call-to-action

# 17

# LONG-FORM TALKS

A long-form talk is an opportunity to go in-depth on a topic and draw the audience into your world for a big impact. We'll talk about the unique structural elements of a long-form talk and how to keep the audience listening the whole time.

## The benefits of a long-form talk

A long-form talk is generally between thirty and sixty minutes long, and we'll focus on this length here, although these talks can be even longer if you're giving a lecture or workshop.

This brings several benefits:

- **You have more time to breathe**
  You can take longer strategic pauses to let points sink in. If you forget something for a moment, you won't feel rushed to recall it.

- **You can cover more points, in more depth, with more stories.**
  Ultimately, the audience will learn more. You can share more than one or two takeaways and use more stories and backup points to illustrate them.

- **You can get the audience to participate**
  You'll have opportunities to engage the audience, ask questions, and answer questions.

We'll talk more about how to make the most of your long-form talk with some specific strategies for talk development and audience engagement with this format. Let's start by looking at the high-level flow of your presentation.

## How to structure a long-form talk

There is a lot going on in a long-form talk, so it's natural to feel overwhelmed when you set out to create one. We recommend that you take it one step at a time. First, identify the high-level motivation for giving your talk and why the audience wants to listen. Then create an outline following the structure below. (If you've created a lightning-talk-style outline for your topic, you can use it as a way to get started, and then add how-to steps and stories to flesh it out for a long-form talk.)

The outline for a long-form talk can follow this flow:

**Introduction**
*Start with a story or another opener.*

**Preview**
*Motivate the audience to keep listening, and list the takeaways you'll cover.*

**Takeaways**
*Share each takeaway. Include the following:*

- **Motivation**
  *Give the audience a reason to pay attention to this takeaway.*

- **Support**
  *Offer supporting arguments and examples.*

- **Stories**
  *Add example stories to illustrate each point.*

- **Counterpoints**
  *Present opposing arguments, if applicable, to show the audience the big picture.*

- **How-to**
  *If your talk is a how-to, outline the steps your audience needs to take.*

**Conclusion**
*Refer back to the introduction's story if you used one and quickly recap the takeaways.*

**Call-to-action**
*Close with a call-to-action. You can tell the audience how they can engage with your work after the talk (review the Final Ask from Chapter 16).*

**Optional**
*Provide designated Q&A time.*

There are a few differences between this outline and the one for a typical lightning talk. You'll be able to cover more than just one or two takeaways – depending on your talk, you could fit in up to five. You can also have more illustrative stories and examples that are unrelated to one another, because you have the time to set the context for each one and switch over cleanly. And finally, you can include how-tos. Some long-form talks are instructive, so you'll want to carefully consider the action steps your audience needs in order to take what they've learned and apply it in the real world.

If you plan to have a dedicated Q&A session afterward, you'll want to make sure there is plenty of time allocated from your total talk time. We recommend ending the main part of your talk and beginning a Q&A session about two-thirds of the way through. If your talk is scheduled for one hour, that means spending forty minutes on your talk and twenty minutes on Q&A.

## Make deeper points

In a long-form talk, you can develop a position around each of your takeaways and use many illustrative stories and examples to drive them home. You can follow this structure for each takeaway:

- Introduce your point.

- Provide motivation by explaining why listening to this takeaway will be important for the audience.

- Present support for your argument and highlight counter-points (more on these below).

- Provide an example or a story to help people understand and remember your point. In a long-form talk, you usually have the room to share a new story for each point. Or, you can use the Slow Reveal Technique and base your entire talk around one overarching story, revealing a little more with each section of your talk. (Note: You don't always have to use stories, but you do want to have evidence to bolster your point, whether it's from personal experience or data from scientific research.)

Long-form talks also allow you to include counterpoints. A counterpoint is a viewpoint in direct opposition to the one you are presenting. The reason you want to present these is that they educate your audience that there are different opinions out there, but leave it up to them to judge an issue. Audiences prefer having all the information to make decisions for themselves, and intentionally leaving out counterpoints can make your presentation seem biased.

Taking a little time to present counterpoints alongside your main points shows your audience that you care about educating them. If you don't present counterpoints, you should at least be prepared for audience members to bring them up (usually during Q&A) and ask you what you think.

## Signpost to keep pace

In Chapter 10, we explained how to signpost with gestures, like using your fingers to indicate a progression from your first point to your second to your third and so on.

Here, we're talking about another form of signposting. This one is verbal and should span the entirety of your talk, not just a small series of steps within it. It's important to try it because in a long-form talk it's easy for the audience to tune out and get lost, and it's easy for you to meander because you know you have a longer time.

Start your talk with a quick preview of what you're going to talk about. List the takeaways you plan to cover, like an agenda or an overview. As you progress, start each takeaway by stating that you're going to talk about it. "Now I'm going to talk about how to evaluate hosting options." When you're finished explaining all of your takeaways, connect the dots at the very end by quickly reviewing each point. This type of wrap-up keeps your talk tight and reminds people what they learned.

Some people complain that this is dull, or they worry that it's annoying to have to listen to someone tell them what they're going to talk about, then talk about it, then tell them what they talked about. But most people actually need repetition. It's a very useful teaching tactic (remember the "underlining" technique, where you repeat a phrase that summarizes your key message to drive your point home).

## Take time to breathe and plan out pauses

In a long-form talk, you can slow down, pause, and think. This is great for you – it helps you calm down and stay present with your talk. But it also gives your audience time to reflect on what you're saying.

If you're new to this practice, it can be helpful to schedule some pauses at first so you remember to take them. As you go through your outline, find points where you'll want to let a statement or question sink in. You can mark them on your outline so that you remember to practice them at first, and of course, you can add more while you're practicing.

## Encourage the audience to participate

There are many ways to get your audience to take an active role in your long-form talk. Let's start with the Mind Reader Strategy, which we introduced in Chapter 12. As people are walking in the door, you want to ask them what they are hoping to get out of this talk.

We highly recommend using the Mind Reader Strategy for every long-form talk that you do. It might be a little harder to execute if you're in an auditorium or large room where there is a lot of space between you and the audience members as they walk in, but find a way, even if it means arriving extra early and approaching people who are milling around.

As you get feedback from your audience, they may mention things that aren't part of your talk. That's okay, because now you know what to cover in the Q&A. If you find that your talk is entirely different from your audience's interests, then you can keep your talk short and get to the Q&A, where you can address their concerns.

When you start to cover a point during your talk that overlaps with an audience's interest, take a moment to get their attention by saying something like, "My friend in the green shirt, I know you are curious to learn about A/B testing. I'm going to talk about it now, and if anything is confusing, feel free to interrupt and ask me a question."

If you're concerned about time and want to invite fewer interruptions and questions, you can address the audience member after you've covered the point and say something like, "My friend in the blue shirt, you had mentioned you were interested in learning about growth hacking on a budget. Does the material I just covered address your need sufficiently?"

If you do have time, however, you can welcome more engagement by adding, "Do you have a follow-up question?" or "Does anyone else have a follow-up question?"

We recommend spending a couple of minutes to address these questions before moving on. You don't have to do this with every point, but in longer talks, it's important to pause periodically and get the audience to interact.

You can also get the audience to participate with show-of-hands-style questions. Karen often starts her talks with a question to get everyone's attention, such as "Show of hands: How many of you have heard the advice that you should have a mentor, but don't have a clue about how to get one?" (You can review how to cue your audience by raising your hand in the air in the section on gestures in Chapter 10.)

## Sample long-form talks

In Karen's talk at Draper University, "Building Your Street Cred,"[53] she introduces her topic by sharing the stories of women she worked with and the challenges they faced to build their reputation. She spends some time defining what she means by "street cred," then she provides the audience with motivation by explaining why they, as young entrepreneurs, need street cred (along with some compelling stats to prove her point).

Next, check out Poornima's presentation from New Relic's FutureStack14, "What Should Developers Do with Data?"[54] At the start of her talk, she clarifies whom this talk is for and how it will help them with certain projects. Then she introduces herself and previews what she's going to cover in the talk. Notice her slides; they use very little text and have simple designs.

# PRACTICE
## CREATE A LONG-FORM TALK

Create an outline for your long-form talk using your proposal from Chapter 6 if you completed it. Jot down the following elements:

1. **Introduction**
   Start with a story or another opener.

2. **Preview**
   Motivate the audience to keep listening, then list the takeaways you'll cover.

3. **Takeaways**
   Share each takeaway and add the following elements.

   - **Motivation**
     Give the audience a reason to pay attention to this specific takeaway.

   - **Support**
     Offer supporting arguments and examples.

   - **Stories**
     Add stories or examples to illustrate the point.

# PRACTICE CONTINUED

- **Counterpoints**
  Present opposing arguments, if applicable, to show your audience the big picture.

- **How-to**
  If your talk is a how-to, outline the steps your audience needs in order to take action.

4. **Conclusion**
   Refer back to the introduction's story if you used one and quickly recap the takeaways.

5. **Call-to-action**
   Tell the audience how they can engage with your work.

Next, mark milestones in your outline to engage your audience:

- Find places to signpost your progress with short recaps of what you just discussed and previews of what you will share next.

- Mark strategic pauses, letting you take a breath and giving the audience time to reflect on your words.

# PRACTICE CONTINUED

- Identify good places to step back and engage the audience by asking them a question or discussing an audience member's specific question (uncovered with the Mind Reader Strategy).

Once you have an outline, work through Chapter 7 to flesh out the content of your talk and practice it. If you're having trouble filling up your entire time target, remember that in a long-form talk, you add more stories and details to support your points.

# RECAP

## CHAPTER 17

## A long-form talk is usually thirty to sixty minutes long

Long-form talks let you make more points in depth, but you'll need to keep the audience engaged the entire time. Try these tactics:

- Signposting
- Strategic pauses and clear transitions
- Audience participation
- The Mind Reader Strategy

## The structure of a long-form talk:

1. Introduction
2. Preview of takeaways
3. Explanation of takeaways
   - In-depth content: motivation, support, stories, counterpoints, and how-to instructions when applicable.
4. Conclusion
5. Call-to-action

# 18

## PANELS

If you feel like you need a baby step to get started with public speaking, consider being a guest on a panel. They're a great way to get more comfortable - after all, you're sharing the stage with others, and there is safety in numbers. And if you're an experienced speaker, you can also benefit from being on a panel (or moderating one).

We love them because they are less strenuous than preparing a full talk and presenting it alone, yet they still give us the opportunity to share our stories, learn from the other speakers, and engage the audience openly.

Now, even though panels require less advance work than a solo talk, you still need to prepare, whether you're a panelist or the moderator. Don't shirk, because it shows. We've felt trapped by plenty of boring panels in which the introductions are long-winded and it's clear the panelists lack rapport. It seems like they all just stepped onstage and met for the first time. Meanwhile, the moderator just can't seem to keep the conversation humming along. We ask ourselves, "If I leave now, will anyone notice?" and can't help but wonder whether we're missing out on some hallway conversations.

Luckily, we've also been to captivating panels where we learned a lesson from each speaker. We've figured out what moderators and panelists need to do to be successful and have tested the techniques ourselves.

Keep in mind that panels come in all shapes and sizes. Here, we'll talk about a common type of panel where a moderator guides the panelists as they share stories about their experiences. Other panels have each speaker give a mini-speech on a topic before answering audience questions. If your panel has a different makeup, you should still be able to pick up some tips.

## How to be a great panelist

Your goal as a panelist is to keep the audience entertained and impart knowledge that helps them with their problems, just as you would during any talk. There are three things you need to do for the best experience possible: prepare your stories, mind your body language, and engage with the audience and other panelists.

### Prepare your stories

As we mentioned before, the great thing about being on a panel is that you don't need to prepare nearly as much as you would for a talk. You'll mostly be sharing first-person experiences and a few lessons that resulted. Ahead of time, you'll know the theme of the panel, and you may even receive a list of questions from your moderator along with a description of the target audience. Armed with that information, you can start to think about the takeaways you want to share with the audience and the stories that will help you illustrate them.

We recommend creating an outline for the points you want to make. Practice them using the Get By with a Little Help from Your Friends Method from Chapter 8 or by recording yourself to get comfortable with the material and identify improvements you can make.

Since you don't control the flow of a panel in the same way as your own monologue talk, you may not be able to get through all your takeaways and stories. But the more prepared you are with anecdotes, the better the overall conversation will flow, thanks to you.

So, what makes a good panel story? First, don't be shy about sharing your failures and what you learned from them. Just like with any talk, the audience wants to learn from your mistakes so they can fast-track their own learning.

Second, controversy makes for fantastic, memorable panels. Whenever possible, surprise the audience with a story that's unexpected, perhaps because you took a less-traveled path or experienced an unusual turn of events.

Not too long ago, Karen was invited to speak on a panel for moms who were considering returning to the workforce after taking a leave of absence to raise their children. She was surprised at the invitation because she hadn't taken time off after having her kids. She even pushed back, but the moderator insisted she be a panelist. At the event, Karen realized why. The moderator wanted to illustrate the different paths the women took with their careers and what they learned along the way. While the other panelists had taken time off because of their children, Karen's story was the unexpected one. And even though she didn't have specific strategies for returning to work, she was able to discuss the challenges of staying current in the tech industry, strategies for embracing social media, and ways to leverage and grow your network, all of which were helpful to the moms in the audience.

Another way to introduce some controversy is to provide counter-points to a commonly held belief.

*Whenever I'm invited to be a panelist, I don't want to be a warm body in a row of other warm bodies. I want to stand out and be memorable. The best way to do that is through myth busting. Before the panel, I'll think about a belief that people in the audience are likely to hold and speak against it.*

*I was recently on a panel about technical recruiting for startups. I decided to have my takeaways debunk the myth that you have to recruit within Silicon Valley and build a team locally. I presented a contrarian view: you should consider recruiting outside Silicon Valley, and that the future of software development lies in learning how to run a remote and distributed team.*

*I made the point that when you recruit in Silicon Valley, you're really limited to the talent pool and have to compete against the likes of Facebook, Google, and other tech giants.*

*I also talked about how people often worry about accountability when running a remote team, but I argued that it's easy to know whether technical work has been completed or not; there are plenty of tools out there to track people's progress. This system also reveals the hires who are skilled at written communication and capable of getting things done on their own.*

*My contrarian view and the points I had prepared left a lasting impression on the audience. I had a number of folks come up to me afterward and ask for more strategies on how to recruit remote workers.*

## Mind your body language

As panelists, we dread walking into the event and seeing a row of stools on the stage. It can be hard to seat ourselves gracefully on a stool, especially if we're on the short side or wearing a skirt or dress. In 2011, Lady Gaga encountered this very situation when she visited Google for a town hall meeting. Wearing ultra-high heels and a short skirt, she could barely get herself seated on the stool for the interview. She quickly joked, "Google chairs are a little high," which broke the awkwardness around the obvious challenge.[55]

Whether you're seated on stools or in chairs, wearing trousers or rocking a great skirt, think about what the audience is seeing. If your legs are bare, keep your feet firmly on the ground or on the stool footrest. (This is easier said than done, because of a natural inclination to cross our legs, but we do try to be mindful of it.)

If the seat has armrests, use them. You'll look and feel more powerful by "filling" your chair instead of putting your hands on your lap.

When the moderator asks you a question, look directly at them, and then when you answer, look at the audience and be confident in your delivery. Remind yourself that the moderator is asking the question on behalf of the audience and that she wants you to share your expertise or opinion with the audience, not just with her. Karen was on a panel recently where one of the panelists directed her answer back to the moderator, and through her vocal inflection, subtly asked for validation that her answer was acceptable. Let's just say it was less than powerful.

## Engage with the audience and other panelists

During the panel, you want to be energetic. Make sure you smile and never, ever look bored when the other panelists are speaking. Your eyes should be on whoever is speaking: the moderator, another panelist, or the audience member asking a question. If you're looking somewhere else, the audience may notice and wonder what they're missing, which is distracting.

Pay attention to what the other panelists are saying so that you can refer to their answers to build on them in one of your responses, or if you're aiming for some controversy, to politely disagree with them. Be curious about your co-panelists' experiences and tailor your stories accordingly. Engage the audience and the other panelists with show-of-hands questions. And above all, have fun.

## How to be a great moderator

Moderating a panel is a great way to demonstrate your thought leadership and expertise on a topic without having to create a full presentation. It can lead to invitations to moderate more panels or speak at other events. We also like that it can be a "forcing function" for you to research and prepare your perspective on an area you haven't spoken about yet.

For example, when Karen was asked to moderate a panel on women leading innovation, she found herself reading about the Innovator's Dilemma, why it can be challenging to be innovative within a successful company, and about the disclaimers tech companies make about innovation in their filing papers before going public. (Google, Zynga, and others warned that their pace of innovation could go down after their IPO as the company grew due to the influx of capital.) She enjoyed her findings so much that she started off the panel discussion that day by sharing what she had learned.

We've moderated panels on topics ranging from strategic leadership to technical innovation to gender diversity. With each one, we've learned and improved. If you're asked to moderate a panel, or want to propose one for a conference, we've got some great tips for you.

## Assemble the panelists and collect their stories

- **Choose panelists with different perspectives**
  Ideally, they'll have opposing viewpoints or varied experiences. If the panelists have already been chosen, ask the organizer to explain why they were chosen and how their perspectives and experiences differ.

- **Meet ahead of time**
  Get your panelists together in person, by phone, or with your favorite conferencing technology. Your goal for this meeting is twofold:

  - **Get to know the panelists**
    Have them introduce themselves and take notes so that you can introduce them at the start of the panel.

  - **Collect their stories**
    Ask them to share stories that fit with the theme for the panel. Push them to talk about first-person experiences and to stay away from general advice. While they're talking, take lots of notes. You'll use these notes to identify which stories you want them to share on panel day, along with overarching themes for the stories.

## Create your game plan

- **Write your panelists' introductions**
  Ask your panelists to send you their bios. Supplementing them with the notes you took during the meeting, create a brief introduction for each panelist. Identify two or three key things to mention about them, including why they are qualified to speak on your panel.

- **Think of an introductory question**
  You'll ask this question after you're finished introducing all the panelists, and each one will answer it in turn. Your goals are to help the panelists become comfortable with speaking by giving them an easy question to answer and to help the audience get used to the speaking voices and any accents. The ideal question relates to the topic at hand and is a little unexpected, to add some intrigue. For example, when Karen moderated a panel on career paths for women, her introductory question was, "What do you do to give back to the women-in-tech community?" For a panel on wearable tech, the introductory question could be, "What feature do you want on your next smartwatch that no one will ever build?"

- **Curate the stories and organize them into themes**
  Using the notes you took during the meeting, look for themes and organize the stories accordingly. For example, in Karen's career path panel, the themes that emerged included "Embracing Risk," "Owning Mistakes," "Promoting Yourself," "Never Stop Networking," and "Trusting Your Gut."

  Group your panelists' stories under these themes and order them so that each person has a chance to speak a couple of times over the course of the panel. Decide which stories to cut, such as ones that are so similar to other stories that they won't add anything to the audience's learning. Then, order the themes with the most interesting, novel, or important stories first, because the ones toward the bottom will be cut if you run out of time.

- **Prepare an introductory lesson for each theme**
  As you progress through your panel, you will introduce each theme and then ask questions that elicit the panelists'

stories. During a theme introduction, we like to grab the audience's attention with some background, research, or other takeaway about the topic. For example, as Karen introduced the "Embracing Risk" theme, she summarized recent NASDAQ research that found that, while women and men can equally evaluate risk in the stock market, women tend to be more pessimistic that the risk will result in a big payout, so they tend to be more conservative. She then connected it to the panel by saying, "It makes me wonder if women in tech are equally pessimistic about career risks ever paying off. Now, let's hear from our panelists about how they've embraced risk."

- **Add some suspense**
  What can you ask the panelists that will reveal something surprising or unexpected? Imagine you were in that audience. What question would cause you to lean forward in your seat and open your mouth in surprise?

The best moderators can ask these questions in a respectful yet direct way, without making their panelists squirm. For inspiration, we like to listen to Terry Gross on NPR's *Fresh Air*.[56]

When Poornima moderated a panel of angel investors in front of an audience of entrepreneurs, she asked, "What's the number one thing that a startup founder has done or said that made you lose interest in them immediately?"

 *I was recently invited to moderate a panel on startup fundraising. The panelists were angel investors from New York City.*

*I knew the audience would be primarily composed of entrepreneurs who were eager to know what it really takes*

to woo an investor. I figured most of the entrepreneurs had heard the usual fluff around investors looking for passionate people who can hustle, and I wanted them to take away real insights they could use as they fundraised for their startup. So, my goal as the moderator was to draw out juicy responses from each investor on the panel.

I started out slowly by asking each investor to share their background, talk about their investment thesis, and describe how often they invest. Once they were warmed up, I cut out all the fluff and put the investors on the spot with a charged introductory question: "What's the number one thing that a startup founder has done or said that made you lose interest in them immediately?"

The rest of my questions got them to reveal their real-life experiences, like concrete examples of how they had helped actual companies, as well as mistakes they had made in their careers. Most of them candidly shared how they had passed up deals they wish they hadn't or lost money pursuing companies in industries they knew very little about. It humanized the panelists and made the entrepreneurs in the audience realize that if an angel chose not to invest in them, it wasn't the end of the world.

To keep the momentum through the very end of the panel, I did a final lightning round of questions. Each panelist could only give a one-word response of the first word that popped into their mind. For example, I asked, "What is the future of tech investing?" and also asked some yes or no questions like, "Are we in a tech bubble?" Limiting their answers to one word pushed them to be raw and reveal what they were really thinking. Lightning rounds like this keep the audience and the panelists at *the edges of their seats because they don't know what you'll ask and no one in the room will be able to predict what the responses will be. And they fuel Q&A because the audience will want to know the reasoning behind the one-word responses.*

### Create one slide to project during the panel

It should contain the title of the panel and the pictures and names of each panelist, along with the company or organization they're affiliated with. We also like to include their Twitter handles and a Twitter hashtag the audience can use for live tweeting.

During your panel, make sure the panelists sit in the same order as they are shown in the slide. This will help orient the audience as the panelists speak. It will also help the audience direct their questions to the right person during the Q&A. Instead of saying, "I have a question for the woman from Femgineer," they can easily refer to her by name.

## Prepare the panelists

### Communicate your game plan

At least a week before, give your panelists a rundown of your panel structure. Let them know that you'll kick off the panel by introducing them and then asking an introductory question that they will each be expected to answer (if you like, you can share it in advance). Tell them about the themes you'll be covering and the stories you want them to share for each theme. We like to do this by creating an outline of the themes and hints about each story. Here's an example of what one theme might look like in such an outline.

> ### Theme: Promoting Yourself
> - *Maria's story about being clear about what you're looking for*

- *Jane's story about advocating for yourself during a promotion cycle*

- *Saanvi's story about engaging a sponsor who helped with a career move*

**Ask them to chime in after another panelist only if they disagree**
Software engineer and speaker Cate Huston describes[57] a panel she was on in which she was asked to only weigh in on a topic if she disagreed with the previous speaker. Consider this tactic to make the discussion more lively and engaging.

**Remind them of the location, date, and time**
Send calendar invites and emails. Over-communicate the details.

**Ask them to arrive early**
Convene your panelists fifteen minutes before the event starts. Your goal is to make sure they meet each other before going onstage and have a chance to chat. You'll also want to review your game plan and answer questions, if they have any.

If you have the opportunity to do so, get them together for a group meal beforehand so they have more time to get to know each other.

## Run the panel smoothly

### Know your place
As the moderator, your role is to make the panel interesting and well-paced without dominating the conversation. While you can add value by interjecting some relevant data and connecting ideas that the panelists have brought up, you need to remember you're not one of the panelists. Make them shine, and you will shine as well.

### Manage your time well
Keep track of time, and abandon stories or questions that are less important as you get near the end of the main portion of the panel.

You want to make sure there is plenty of time for questions. We recommend moving to audience Q&A about two-thirds of the way through the time allocated for the panel. If your panel is scheduled for one hour, that means spending forty minutes on the panelists' stories and twenty minutes on Q&A.

## Master the Q&A portion

During audience Q&A, your job as the moderator is to accommodate as many questions as possible and to help make sure all of the panelists are included. Repeat the questions if you don't have microphones for your audience to use. Rephrase them if you can add more meaning or make them more concise.

As a general rule of thumb, don't answer questions yourself. Step in only if the panelists can't answer the question, and only if you have something valuable to share. Consider using the Crowdsource Strategy by asking, "Can anyone in the audience answer that question?"

Since you want all of the panelists to answer questions, you might feel a little short on time. You may have to cut off someone who is asking a long-winded question. While not always easy, you need to step in and let the person know that you understand the question. Interrupt with a polite but firm "I hear you" or "I bet our panelists know exactly what you're talking about; let's see what they have to say." If the person still insists on talking, stand up, approach the audience, and make a "T" with your hands – the universal time-out sign. Chances are the person will get the message.

As you approach the end of the allotted time, let the audience know. For example, you could say, "We have time for one or two more questions" or "This will be the last question."

Thank the panelists. You can do this before or after the Q&A. Keep it brief. All you need is a simple "Please join me in thanking our panelists," then clap your hands so that the audience knows to join in.

Enjoy! During the panel, be sure to smile. Be energetic and enthusiastic! With all the prep work that you've done, you'll have a good time as the moderator.

## Sample panels

Inspirefest 2015 hosted a lively "Investor Panel"[58] in which the panelists did a great job taking a stance and defending their views on the issue of venture funding for women entrepreneurs in the US. Notice the conversational rapport between the moderator and speakers, and pay attention to the body language of the different panelists while they're speaking and listening. Where are they looking? Which ones appear to be the most engaged?

In this "Women in Technology Panel"[59] at FedTalks 2014, the moderator briefly introduces each panelist and then opens the discussion with a series of shocking statistics.

The moderator of an Internet Week 2013 panel titled "How Women Are Engaging with Technology"[60] takes a different opening approach by allowing the panelists to introduce themselves. She then kicks off the conversation with a question for the speakers about the best and worst instances of tech products designed with women in mind.

# RECAP

## CHAPTER 18

### How to be a great panelist:

- Prepare in advance. Come ready with personal stories and crisp takeaways. Practice them with the **Get By with a Little Help from Your Friends Method.**

- Add suspense by presenting controversial viewpoints. And if you disagree with another panelist, say so (respectfully).

- While you're onstage, be thoughtful about your body language and pay attention to whoever is speaking.

### How to be a great panel moderator:

- Prepare your panelists in advance. Meet with them to collect their stories, then prioritize and organize stories into themes. Share your game plan with the panelists.

- While you're onstage, keep the panel humming along smoothly. Keep track of time and let the panelists shine.

- Don't be afraid to ask questions that elicit controversy or surprising answers.

# 19

# WEBINARS AND PODCASTS

These days, you can give a talk to an audience of hundreds or even thousands of people without leaving your home.

A webinar is a talk that's broadcast online in real time and can reach people all around the world. Viewers can watch it live and even participate, and you can also record the event and publish it online afterward.

Another way to distribute your talk online is to record a podcast, which is an audio-only recording that you create and publish to reach more people. With podcasts, the audience members can't listen in real time, interact with you, or see slides, but it's a great way to appeal to people who want control over when and where they hear your talk, as well as pause and rewind.

Let's talk about how to adapt your talk for webinar and podcast formats, starting with how to host a webinar.

## How to ace a webinar

### Webinar hosting
Webinar hosting options include Google Hangouts On Air,[61] which is free, and GoToWebinar,[62] which is a paid product (although it offers a free trial). GoToWebinar lets your audience register for the

webinar with their email address, which then gives you the ability to message viewers via email before and after the webinar, which is helpful for sending reminders and presentation assets. Both platforms support hundreds of viewers.

Check whether your webinar hosting platform lets you record your webinar for later use. If it doesn't, use your own screen recording software. TechSmith has a useful guide[63] on how to record webinars with its software, including free trial versions. Camtasia[64] is a popular option.

### Webinar format

In our experience, most webinars last for an hour. You can treat it like a long-form talk and split your time between speaking and Q&A. A sixty/forty (speaking/Q&A) split works well, but even a fifteen/forty-five split can work if your audience is engaged enough to ask forty-five minutes' worth of questions.

Recently we gave a webinar on how to appeal to your audience during a talk, and we spoke for about fifteen minutes and had nearly forty-five minutes allocated for questions, which our audience took advantage of.

### How to host webinar Q&A

You can structure your webinar Q&A in one of two ways, or a combination of the two:

- Collect all audience questions in advance, then read them out loud during your webinar's Q&A session one at a time and answer them.

- Solicit questions during the live webinar.

Both of these methods will go smoothly if you make sure that there's plenty to talk about during Q&A. Gather questions ahead of your webinar with an online version of the Mind Reader Strategy from Chapter 12. For example, you can email your audience members and ask them to tweet their questions earlier in the day of your presentation, using a hashtag for the webinar, or you can create an online form (e.g., with Google Docs surveys[65]) where they can submit questions. If someone is organizing your webinar for you or partnering with you, ask them to help circulate the Q&A instructions to the people they've invited.

Once you get to the Q&A section of your talk, you can kick it off by reading and answering a few questions you gathered ahead of time. If you're soliciting questions from your audience live during the Q&A, there may be lulls, so you can use the prepared questions to fill the time and inspire audience members to ask their own.

For a live audience Q&A, you can have audience members submit questions on your webinar hosting platform's chat dialogue, if it comes with one. We also recommend Twitter or Chatroll,[66] because they're easy to use. One bonus of using Twitter for Q&A is that it's a social network; people who didn't attend your talk but are in your audience members' Twitter networks will see the activity, meaning that your talk will get more exposure. Give your audience clear instructions on how the interactive Q&A will work, ideally both emailing them before the webinar and then reiterating the instructions once it starts. For example, if you're using Twitter, give them instructions on how to log on to Twitter, write a question, and tag it with a special hashtag[67] to make sure you see it.

It can be a little tough to juggle an interactive Q&A because you need to check for questions while answering others on camera. If you're not comfortable with this, you can ask a friend, colleague, or audience member ahead of time to be your volunteer Q&A manager. They can pre-screen questions and then feed you the ones they select.

Note that you don't need to limit audience questions to the Q&A session if your webinar is casual enough to accommodate questions mid-talk and you feel comfortable switching back and forth between your presentation and the questions.

## Webinar quality

Since webinars use video as a medium, you'll need to make sure the audio and the visuals of your face or slides are clear. Always do a test run before your webinar, with a friend watching as an audience member from a different location. Check for these elements:

- Lighting
  There should be plenty of natural light shining on your face. If you aren't near a window, then get a lamp that supplies white light. Avoid backlighting (where your light source is behind you) because it will cast shadows on your face.

- Internet speed
  Ask the friend who's watching your webinar whether the video is lagging. If you find that your internet speed is slow, you can start by quitting applications that are using a lot of bandwidth. Any application that is uploading or downloading data will slow down your video. If your internet is still slow after you shut down applications, then consult with your internet service provider (you might have to upgrade your speed) or find a more reliable internet source.

- Sound
  Project your loudest voice and your quietest voice to make sure the sound is balanced. We also recommend wearing a headset or using a standalone microphone to sound clear and reduce ambient noise. Do your best to find a quiet spot

away from other people and noises. It can be quite distracting for audience members, especially those with sensitive hearing.

- **Eye contact**
  When you speak, look directly into the camera. Make sure that your friend pays attention to how often your eyes stray. When your gaze is at an angle, like if you're watching yourself speak on the screen, it can throw people off (unless you're giving a webinar with a partner, where you can look at them while they're speaking or reading incoming questions).

- **Slides**
  If you plan on presenting slides, test them to make sure you can flip through them while the webinar is live. Make sure you find a way to show your face, as well as your slide deck, because the audience needs to see your face in order to connect with you. Most webinar hosting platforms have options for showing both video and slides or switching between the two.

Before a webinar, always set up your computer and test the sound and video quality. Here's a guide.

# PRACTICE
## PREP FOR A WEBINAR

*Involves asking others for feedback (optional).*

Improve the quality of your online presentation with good lighting, sound, and eye contact.

1. **Revisit your talk from the practice in Chapter 2: the story of your favorite dessert**
   You are going to use the same story to complete this activity.

2. **Set up your laptop in a quiet area where you plan to host your webinar**
   If you already know which webinar hosting service you want to use, use it to practice. Otherwise, you can simulate how you will appear on the webinar by using a recording service like Mac's Photo Booth.

3. **Record yourself giving your short dessert talk.**
   Pay attention to and improve the following elements:

   • **Lighting**
     Make sure there is enough light shining on your face by turning on additional light sources if need be. Avoid backlighting that casts shadows on your face.

# PRACTICE CONTINUED

- **Sound**
  Find a quiet spot to record, wear a headset to improve the sound quality, and make sure to test both your loudest and your quietest voice before producing the recording.

- **Eye contact**
  Look into the camera as you are delivering your talk.

- **Slide progression (if you're practicing with webinar hosting software)**
  Make sure your slides show up and advance at the right time (with no significant lag). Ensure that the audience can see your face for most of your talk, even if you use slides.

4. **Check the quality of your recording**
   You can ask a friend to watch it and give feedback on the lighting, sound, eye contact, and slides. If you're using webinar hosting software to practice, invite them to the webinar so they can check conditions while you are speaking.

## How to record a podcast

You can record an audio-only version of your talk and distribute it as a podcast for people who prefer to listen to talks through headphones at home or on their morning commutes. Podcasts are not live streams like webinars, so you have more control over your recording. Popular podcast distribution methods include Sound-Cloud[68] and iTunes.[69]

- **Sound quality**
  With podcasts, sound is everything. Listeners are pretty sensitive because they're using only one sense, unlike in a live presentation or webinar. So be wary of any and all ambient noise and fidgety movements - even jewelry clinking can make strange noises.

  We highly recommend that you use a standalone microphone or a headset mic when recording podcasts. Don't rely on the built-in mic on your laptop or computer, as it will reduce the quality of the podcast recording. And just like with a webinar, always do a test run to check for sound quality.

- **Using your voice**
  Remember those vocal inflections from Chapter 10? Those are important when podcasting because you can't rely on visual cues to help get your message across. You can use inflections to evoke an emotional response and provide visual imagery. Even using pauses and sighs can create a dramatic effect. When you practice your talk for a podcast, think about your choice of words, your tone, and the impact you'd like your vocal delivery to make on the listener.

A podcast is a unique medium because you can look anywhere you want during the presentation, meaning you can keep your eye on an outline to help you stay on track (which is especially helpful if you are hosting with another presenter on the podcast because it keeps both of you in sync). Just make sure not to create noise by interacting with it, whether it's on paper or your computer screen.

## Provide supplementary information

With podcasts, people won't always pick up on everything you say, and you want them to be able to fill in the gaps in their understanding or learn more later. It's helpful to provide supplementary information in the podcast's description or notes section that links to any resources or websites you mentioned in the recording.

We also recommend adding show notes (an outline of what you talked about) or a transcript. The transcription service Rev[70] can create the transcript for you for a fee if you don't want to type it up yourself; just send them your podcast recording and they'll give you a text file to accompany it. You can even get the transcript time-stamped so that users can find a point in the transcript and then jump to that exact moment in your audio recording.

# RECAP

## CHAPTER 19

### Webinars are live-streamed online video presentations

- Typical webinars last an hour with a portion of that dedicated to Q&A, but you can use any structure you like.

- You can host Q&A live or prepare it beforehand by soliciting audience questions via email or a survey.

- Always test lighting and sound before going live.

### Podcasts are audio-only recordings (not live)

- Your voice is your main tool, so make sure it's expressive.

- Test sound quality and avoid ambient noise.

- In the podcast's description or notes section, provide links to resources you mention in the recording. You can also share a summary, show notes, or a transcript.

# BONUS
## BECOME A MEETING MAVEN

You might be wondering why a book on public speaking would have a chapter on meetings.

Here's the thing. The first time many of us speak in public in a professional setting is in a meeting. Perhaps we pose a question or share a status update. Or walk through a project we just completed. Or pitch an idea for something new. And being a great public speaker makes you an effective communicator in meetings, whether they're one-on-ones with your manager, small group meetings, or customer visits.

We'll kick things off with tips on how to run a work meeting or be a guest presenter at one. Then, we'll talk about how to get what you want in a meeting, because unlike a traditional one-way presentation, meetings often involve making a request of your teammates and supervisors.

**How to be a confident communicator in your next meeting**

## Create a compelling agenda

Meeting agendas are a lot like proposals for talks. You want to be clear about your intended audience, the takeaways you want to share, and any calls-to-action.

---

If you want a VIP to attend your meeting, you'll need a crisp, compelling agenda to convince them to attend. Or, if you're proposing an agenda item for a meeting that someone else is organizing, a persuasive proposal can help convince them to include your topic in their overall agenda. And sometimes you'll be invited to speak at a meeting, perhaps to give an update on a project you've been working on. By creating an agenda for what you'll cover, you can clarify their expectations and be confident you'll be addressing the right information.

For important meetings, you'll need to think through what you plan to say and even practice it. You can use your agenda as a starting point for the outline of what you'll cover in the meeting, just as you would use a talk proposal to develop your presentation. Refer back to an agenda as you practice what you'll say in a meeting to make sure you're staying on course and achieving what you originally set out to do.

Agendas have elements similar to those in a persuasive proposal. Come up with a catchy title, a summary of what you'll cover, the take-aways, and why you're the person to speak about it. Here's an example.

> *Meeting Invitation: The analytics that got us here ain't going to get us there.*
>
> *To date, we've been doing a decent job with measuring and analyzing our site traffic. It's helped us grow our business to $5M in annual revenue in just a year. Yet, our approach is not the right one for growing our business to the next level. In this meeting, I'll cover:*

> - *The tools we use today and the business decisions we make using the data we collect*
> - *The business decisions we need to make in the next twelve months*
> - *My recommendations for a new analytics tool to meet our needs*
> - *The budget we'll need*
>
> *As you may remember, I have a master's in Data Science and Analytics, and helped grow my previous company to become a market leader. I'm looking forward to doing the same here!*

## Know your audience

Just like with a talk, you want to know who will be attending the meeting and what's important to them. Do your homework to find out what they need right now, their business challenges, and how your presentation can help them with their goals.

Remember the Mind Reader Strategy? We highly recommend using it in meetings where you're just not sure what to expect from the other attendees, how to direct the conversation, or where in the agenda to spend the bulk of your time. At the start of the meeting, or as people are arriving, ask them about their goals for the meeting. What are they hoping to get out of it? What decisions do they want to make?

This can work in meetings with colleagues, but we've also used this strategy many times in customer meetings. Whether you're dealing with a prospect or a loyal customer, it's good practice to take the time to ask them what they want to get out of the meeting. This helps you focus your time on what matters to them, and more importantly, to keep their attention.

The Mind Reader Strategy can also be helpful when dealing with other departments or teams. Take the time to understand their goals, and then have an exploratory conversation where you look for alignment.

## Think about your style

Review Chapter 10 and think about how you want to deliver your talk. What style will be most effective with your audience? Should you be casual or formal? How will you use your body and voice to convey your points?

## Practice

You knew this was coming. We recommend that you practice what you want to say ahead of the meeting, initially with an outline and then without it. Record yourself, watch it, and make adjustments until you are confident about your message and your delivery.

Consider assembling a mini-audience of colleagues to get feedback on your presentation, especially if the meeting is with a large group or if it's the first time you're presenting this material. You'll get valuable feedback and gain a few supporters within your company because they will be "in the know" before the meeting takes place.

## Create stunning slides (or go without)

Some company cultures depend on and expect slides at every meeting. Others may want them only for making decisions and not for things like status updates. Figure out what's appropriate for your meeting by asking the organizer. Or, if you're presenting to a customer, ask your sales rep what's expected.

Revisit Chapter 11 for best practices for creating slides, all of which apply to meetings as well. And we offer the same cautions for meetings as we do for talks. Create slides after you have finished your agenda or pitch and practiced what you're going to say. You won't be distracted by creating slides while preparing, and you'll be prepared to speak at the meeting if technical glitches prevent you from using slides. You also won't need to use them as prompts.

## Prepare for challenging questions

Prepare for challenging questions in advance by brainstorming possible questions by yourself or with colleagues. Then review the strategies for handling tough questions in Chapter 12: the Crowd-source Strategy involves the audience in answering questions that stump you, and the Take It Offline Strategy prevents a complicated question from taking over your session.

## Last but not least, strike a power pose

Nerves can strike in meetings just as much as when we walk onto a big stage. Strike a power pose for just two minutes before the meeting to help reduce your anxiety and feel more confident. If nerves are a big concern for you, review the stage fright tips in Chapter 9. They'll help you deal with stage fright and nerves in all kinds of settings, large and small.

## How to make a request and get what you want

You may be thinking, "Sure, presenting information at meetings is a lot like presenting on the big stage. But usually I also need my audience to agree to do something." How can you pitch ideas to a boss, your colleagues, or even a customer and tip the outcome in your favor?

Some requests, or "asks," are easy to make, especially when we've seen someone make a similar request before and be successful, which increases our confidence. Others can be more challenging;

maybe we're not sure whom to ask, whether they'll think negatively about our request, or how we'll get people to agree with our priorities.

Asks can also be large or small. A small one could be something you need to get your job done. Perhaps it's a new computer because you can't run all the apps you need at the same time. Or moving a deadline because you hit some unexpected bugs. Or working remotely to take care of a sick family member. They often start with "All I need is..."

A bigger ask might require a pivot in company focus, a budget commitment, or an improvement to an ingrained process. We'll give you three tips to help you make any ask, and then we'll dive into how to create a more formal pitch for those bigger requests.

### Tip #1: Make it crisp

Be clear and concise about what you are asking for. This tip may seem obvious, but sometimes we get so caught up in the problem that we aren't clear about what we need to be successful. If we're struggling with getting through the bug backlog, we need to think about what would be helpful. A faster computer? An updated license for a tool? A change in the code review process before fixes are checked in? Instead of spending most of your request describing how difficult the problem has been for you, make it crisp and clear about what you need.

Also, if you're asking for something that will require a budget, do your homework and know the amount it will cost. For example, if you're asking for permission to go to a conference, provide an estimate of your travel costs.

### Tip #2: Make it easy for them to say yes

If you frame your request as a trial or put a time limit on it, it's easier for someone to approve it. When Karen was a vice president at a software company, one of the engineers in her department asked for a flexible schedule so that she could work from home every afternoon. It turns out that she was a single mom, and her teenage son was starting to get into trouble after school. This mom wanted to work from home so that she could keep an eye on things. To make it easier for Karen to say yes, she time-boxed her request, asking if she could try out the new schedule for just a month. If it wasn't working out, they could revisit the decision.

Another way to make it easy to green-light an ask is to prepare reasons that will make an impact on the core business. One time, an engineer asked Karen for a new ultra-light laptop that wasn't on the approved equipment list. The engineer anticipated that Karen would push back, so she explained that her enterprise customers were using that model, and she wanted to be able to triage the bugs they were reporting on the same hardware.

In case you're curious, in both cases Karen said yes.

### Tip #3: Don't just ask; make an offer

Not too long ago, Poornima attended a negotiation workshop where they worked in pairs for a role-playing exercise. Person A would ask Person B for something. When it was Poornima's turn to create a request, she set the context for her partner and told him he was a CFO at a tech company. Her pitch went something like this:

> *"Hi, Person B, thanks for taking the time out of your busy schedule today to meet with me.*
>
> *I'm the founder of Femgineer, an education company. For the past two years, we've been running a Lean Product Development Course that has graduated over seventy students around the world.*

*The course is for engineers and tech entrepreneurs, and it teaches them how to transform an idea into a software product. In the course, we advise all our students to use your company's service when they build their products, and they've found it to be really beneficial.*

*In 2015, we'd like to offer scholarships to students who might not be able to afford our program, and I'm here to ask whether you'd be open to providing a $50,000 sponsorship, which we can use to provide our students with scholarships.*

*In exchange for the sponsorship, we'll highlight you as our marquee sponsor, invite you to meet with the students, and continue to highlight how your products and services will benefit our students as they build software products. I know you've got a great base of customers in the US, but this will bring you a lot of exposure in international markets and you will be an important part of our students' success."*

Poornima was winging this and probably would have come up with some hard data if she were asking for something in real life. After she presented her request, the instructor said, "What I like is that you didn't just ask, you made an offer."

Here's what the instructor meant. Too often when we ask for something, we phrase it in a way that is only meant to benefit us. This tendency is tricky to detect, especially if we base our request on something we did to benefit the other person initially. For example,

> *"Over the past quarter, I've reduced the bug count by 50 percent. Clearly my work has benefited the company, and I'm now here to ask for $2,000 to attend a training class."*

A reduced bug count is wonderful, but the recipient has already experienced this benefit. Since it's in the past, it doesn't give a concrete incentive they can enjoy in the future. True, there is an ongoing benefit to this ask, like having an outstanding employee, which can pay off down the road. But the problem is that it's just too subtle.

An offer takes the ask and adds a clear explanation of how the other person is going to benefit. Here's how we can frame our example request within an offer:

> *"As you know, I've been implementing a new process over the past quarter to improve our existing code base. I recently measured its progress and noticed that it reduced the bug count by 50 percent. I also spoke to Jamie in sales, who told me that customers who were originally on the fence about renewing their subscription to our product were thrilled with the quality improvements and have gone on to renew their subscriptions.*
>
> *I'm here to ask for a $2,000 education budget. I actually learned how to implement the new process from a course I took, and now I'd like to take an advanced version that costs $2,000. The advanced course will teach me another process for scaling our code base so that we can service more customers.*

> *Given that the previous improvements have increased renewals, I'm certain we'll continue to see renewals go up in the next couple of months. And if they do, I'm concerned that we'll run into a scaling issue. I've pulled up some stats [show graph of performance], and here you can see for yourself how our performance has gone down with the increased number of customers.*
>
> *Right now, our customers only experience minor slowdowns, but as we grow, our product will no longer be able to support the additional customers. I'm sure you can understand why we're going to need to scale the code base before the next quarter. If we put it off, then we'll lose the renewals we've gained."*

This example comes from the real experience of one of Poornima's mentees. (And yes, he got what he asked for.)

To take this approach, start by setting the context. What did you do in the past, and what were the positive results? Next, make sure that you show causality. In the above example, the customers renewed because of the improvements; it was a direct benefit, not just a correlation.

Finally, present your offer, including an ask and a clear benefit to the other person. Most importantly, getting back to Tip #1, the offer needs to be clear and concise. Not only do you want to make it easy to understand, but you also want to make it easy for someone to share it with their boss or other people who will be involved in the decision-making process. This prevents the offer from getting muddled as it's repeated to others.

Here's a bonus tip. If your offer is rejected, don't slink away with your tail between your legs, which is too often the default response to rejection. Instead, ask the person why they rejected your offer and then use the reason to modify your pitch for a better chance of success.

## Bigger asks: Six elements of a big-idea pitch

What if you have an idea that is so big and important that, to put it into motion, you'll need serious buy-in and a lot of resources? What if you need thousands of dollars or a whole team at your company to switch its focus for three months?

Have no fear. Here is our six-part recipe for a pitch that can bring a larger and more formal idea to the table (and you'll also want to use all the tips we covered so far to present it). Karen sees it used within companies, and it's her go-to approach for writing proposals for consulting work as well.

There are six things to outline when making a serious pitch:

1. Idea
2. Audience
3. Purpose
4. Outcome
5. Process
6. Ask

### 1. Idea

Before we get started, prepare an idea you want to pitch. Is it a new product? A new feature for an existing product? An improved approach to responding to customer feedback or hiring employees? Write down your idea, ideally in fifteen words or less. By limiting

---

the number of words, you force yourself to be crisp. For example, imagine you have an idea for a new feature in your company's social media app. The idea, in fifteen words or less, would be:

> *A new feature that allows users to record the pronunciation of their name.*

## 2. Audience

By now, you know the importance of getting to know your audience for any talk you give. When pitching an idea, you also need to know your audience. Who are you pitching to? Who are the decision makers? If you don't know the target audience and what's important to them, think about who you can ask to figure it out. Don't leave out this important element!

Do your homework to find out what's important to them.

> - *What are their business goals?*
> - *What metrics matter to them?*
> - *What challenges are they facing? Budget cuts? Stiff competition? Employee retention issues?*

In our example above, let's say that the audience is:

> *Jane Doe, the product owner for the social media app. One of Jane's goals is to increase the number of Fortune 500 customers that use the app daily.*

## 3. Purpose

Here's where you describe your idea. What's its purpose? What are you trying to solve? And, if you're building a better mousetrap, why should someone care?

You can also use storytelling to grab your audience's attention and make your idea memorable and relatable. Here's an example of how we could weave a story into the description of our idea to convey the purpose of the pitch:

> *One of our large US customers acquired a firm in Beijing; they asked me if I knew of a resource to help them learn to pronounce their new colleagues' names. I didn't. In fact, I tend to mispronounce names from all cultures, and it's embarrassing. To solve this problem and increase the daily usage of our app, I'm proposing a new feature where users can record their names so others can hear how to pronounce them.*

## 4. Outcome

What is the outcome of your project? Is it a prototype or shipped code? Is it a study or a report? State what you'll be delivering and how you'll measure success. If you want to test a hypothesis, be clear about how you will run a pilot and what you hope to learn from it.

For our example idea, the outcome might be something like this:

> *A prototype design and a report summarizing customer research, including an estimated increase in daily usage because of this feature.*

## 5. Process

Be clear about the process you'll follow for the project, who you'll work with, and the timeframes you'll adhere to. For example:

> *I will run a focus group for twenty US customers and twenty Asia-Pacific customers. I will work with Sophia on the UX team to create a design, which we will review with five partners and revise based on their feedback. Final design will be ready within sixty days of approval.*

## 6. Ask

Last but not least, be clear about what you need. As with the small requests we talked about earlier in this chapter, you want to be crisp and clear with what you are seeking approval for. Perhaps you want permission to investigate a new open source library, the budget to make a purchase, or a head count to work on the project. Whatever it is, be clear.

Back to our example, this is what our ask might be:

> *$25,000 for travel to run focus groups in Q3, and approval to put other projects on hold for sixty days.*

And of course, make sure that your pitch as a whole is framed as an offer more than an ask. Weave elements of the offer throughout your whole pitch after getting in your audience's heads.

### Bring your pitch to life

Once you have identified the six elements of your pitch, create an outline using the activity below.

If you're presenting a bigger pitch in a more formal setting, you can use the techniques we've provided for bringing a talk to life. Talk through and practice your pitch while recording yourself, and it's very helpful to get a mini-audience that can give you feedback, especially if they're coworkers who know the people and projects involved (Chapter 8).

Also think about presentation style: Do you need to create slides, or will a less formal approach work better for your target audience?

When you feel you're ready to make your pitch, don't forget to strike a power pose for two minutes to build your confidence and lower your anxiety. We'll be rooting for you!

# PRACTICE
## CREATE A PITCH FOR AN IDEA

Create a crisp pitch to get buy-in for your idea. Jot down answers to these questions:

1. **Idea**
   What are you pitching, in fifteen words or less?

2. **Audience**
   Who are the decision makers? What are their business goals? What metrics do they track?

3. **Purpose**
   What are you trying to solve? What's the customer's pain point? What's the story as to why this is important?

4. **Outcome**
   What will you deliver? A pilot or a full solution? What will change as a result? How will you measure success?

5. **Process**
   What work will you do for this project? Who will you work with?

6. **Ask**
   What do you need to be successful? Approval to take the next step? Budget? Resources?

# RECAP

## BECOME A MEETING MAVEN

### Public speaking improves your meeting skills

You'll become a more effective communicator with your boss, teammates, and customers.

### If you make a small request, remember these three tips:

- Tip #1: Make it crisp.
- Tip #2: Make it easy for them to say yes.
- Tip #3: Don't just ask; make an offer.

### Bigger asks need a pitch with six parts:

1. Idea
2. Audience
3. Purpose
4. Outcome
5. Process
6. Ask

# EPILOGUE

If you've gone through this whole book, worked through the activities, and created a presentation, then congratulations!

Hopefully your new skills will translate into polished delivery, a deeper connection with your audience, and confidence when presenting – even if you still get butterflies.

We want your strongest takeaways from the book to be the following: it is possible to present abstract and complex ideas in a simple and engaging way, and the end goal is confidence, not perfection.

Be proud of yourself for taking the time to improve your public speaking skills – you've hit a major milestone in your professional life. And you might be wondering, "What's next?"

Find as many ways as you can to practice public speaking. And remember that this book just covers the most common presentation formats and styles, so you still have room to play around with your personal style. Also, think about what new challenges and opportunities you want to take on. Set yourself a stretch goal like giving a keynote, delivering a college commencement, or presenting at TED.

The possibilities are endless.

And whether you're preparing for your first presentation or your one hundredth, we want to hear from you! Tweet @femgineer and share your experience with us.

– Poornima and Karen

# ABOUT THE AUTHORS

Poornima Vijayashanker is the founder of Femgineer, an education startup that helps empower engineers, founders, and product leads to transform their ideas into tangible, high-impact products.

Poornima has been an Entrepreneur-in-Residence at 500 Startups, where she advised startup companies on product development, technical recruiting, customer acquisition, and fundraising. She was also the founding engineer at Mint.com, where she helped build, launch, and scale the product until its acquisition in 2009. She has been a guest lecturer at Duke University's Pratt School of Engineering.

Poornima holds degrees in Electrical and Computer Engineering and Computer Science from Duke University's Pratt School of Engineering. When she's not building products or companies, she enjoys Bikram yoga, rock climbing, and running. She lives in sunny Palo Alto, California, with her fiancé and two cats, Colby Jack and Riley.

Karen Catlin is an advocate for women in the tech industry. She is a leadership coach for women and an advisor to tech companies on improving gender diversity.

Formerly, Karen was a vice president at Adobe Systems, where she led corporate-wide product globalization, software security, and other cross-company functions within the office of the CTO.

Outside of her commercial ventures, Karen works with a number of nonprofits. She's on the Board of Directors of the CLUB, an incubator of women leaders, and through Brown University's Women's Launch Pad, she mentors young women about to start their careers.

In 2015, the California State Assembly honored her with the Wonder Women Tech Innovator Award for her outstanding achievements in business and technology and for being a role model for women.

Karen holds a degree in Computer Science from Brown University. She lives in San Mateo, California, with her husband and their two children. In her spare time, she designs jewelry and knitwear.

# REFERENCES

Visit www.femgineer.com/present-book/interactive-bundle for a clickable list of the notes, images, and videos in this book.

## Introduction

1. Karen Catlin, "Women in Tech: The Missing Force" (presented at TEDx - College of William and Mary, Williamsburg, Virginia, April 6, 2014), https://youtu.be/8uiEHaDSfgI

2. Poornima Vijayashanker, "Taking the Time to Tinker" (presented at TEDxNavesink, Navesink, New Jersey, June 12, 2014), https://youtu.be/XJfdxEuJVdM

3. Femgineer Confident Communicator Course, www.femgineer.com/confident-communicator-course/

4. @femgineer, www.twitter.com/femgineer

5. #presentbook, https://twitter.com/search?q=presentbook

## Chapter 3: Find a Topic

6. Poornima Vijayashanker, "The Evolution of a Scrappy Startup to a Successful Web Service" (presented at Silicon Valley Code Camp, San Jose, California, November 2008), www.slideshare.net/poornimav/the-evolution-of-a-scrappy-startup-to-a-successful-web-service

7. Poornima Vijayashanker, "From Duke to Mint: The Blue She-Devil and Successful Startup" (presented at the BE+K

Innovation and Technology Management Series, Duke University, Durham, North Carolina, June 8, 2010), www.femgineer.com/2010/06/from-duke-to-mint-the-blue-she-devil-and-successful-startup

## Chapter 5: Tell a Story

8. Jerry Seinfeld, Comedian, November 1, 2002, www.imdb.com/title/tt0328962

9. Amy Poehler and Tina Fey, "Tina Fey and Amy Poehler Open the Show," 72nd Annual Golden Globe Awards, January 11, 2015, https://www.youtube.com/watch?v=7N1L2ducpGA

10. Andrew Stanton, "The Clues to a Great Story" (presented at TED2012, Long Beach, California, February 2012), www.ted.com/talks/andrew_stanton_the_clues_to_a_great_s tory

## Chapter 6: Pitch Your Talk

11. Technically Speaking newsletter signup, www.tinyletter.com/techspeak

12. @techspeakdigest, www.twitter.com/techspeakdigest

13. Technical Women Speak Too, https://plus.google.com/u/0/communities/1018180012366 62563704

14. @CallbackWomen, www.twitter.com/CallbackWomen

15. Lanyrd, www.lanyrd.com

16. WikiCFP, www.wikicfp.com

17. Kaliya Hamlin, "unConferencing: How to Prepare to Attend an Unconference," www.unconference.net/unconferencing-how-to-prepare-to-attend-an-unconference

18. Lean Startup Conference, www.leanstartup.co

## Chapter 7: Develop Your Talk

19. Poornima Vijayashanker, "Taking the Time to Tinker" (presented at TEDxNavesink, Navesink, New Jersey, June 12, 2014), https://youtu.be/XJfdxEuJVdM

20. Beth Dunn, "How to Be a Writing God" (presented at INBOUND, Boston, Massachusetts, September 2014), https://youtu.be/S8Q3vnPM6kk

## Chapter 8: Practice

21. Carmine Gallo, "Deliver a Presentation like Steve Jobs," Bloomberg, January 25, 2008, www.bloomberg.com/bw/stories/2008-01-25/deliver-a-presentation-like-steve-jobsbusinessweek-business-news-stock-market-and-financial-advice

## Chapter 9: Get Over Stage Fright

22. Dale Carnegie, The Art of Public Speaking (Project Gutenberg, 2005), www.gutenberg.org/files/16317/16317-h/16317-h.htm

23. Dana Carney, Amy Cuddy, and Andy Yap, "Power Posing: Brief Nonverbal Displays Affect Neuroendocrine Levels and

Risk Tolerance," Psychological Science 21, no. 10 (2010), www.ncbi.nlm.nih.gov/pubmed/20855902

24. Amy Cuddy, "Your Body Language Shapes Who You Are" (presented at TEDGlobal 2012, Edinburgh, Scotland, June 2012), www.ted.com/talks/amy_cuddy_your_body_language_shap es_who_you_are

25. Jin Shin Jyutsu finger mudras, www.balanceflow.com/the-jin-shin-jyutsu-finger-mudras

## Chapter 10: Style Your Talk

26. The Public Speaker podcast, www.lisabmarshall.com/publicspeaker

27. Monica Lewinsky, "The Price of Shame" (presented at TED2015, Vancouver, Canada, March 2015), www.ted.com/talks/monica_lewinsky_the_price_of_shame

28. Howcast, "How to Project Your Voice on Stage," www.howcast.com/videos/315121-how-to-project-your-voice-on-stage

## Chapter 11: Create Stunning Slides

29. Slidebean, www.slidebean.com

30. iStock, www.istockphoto.com

31. Bigstock, www.bigstockphoto.com

32. Unsplash, www.unsplash.com

33. Scott Hanselman, "11 Top Tips for a Successful Technical Presentation," May 17, 2008, www.hanselman.com/blog/11TopTipsForASuccessfulTechnicalPresentation.aspx

34. Brené Brown, "The power of vulnerability" (presented at TED2010, Long Beach, California, June 2010), www.ted.com/talks/brene_brown_on_vulnerability

35. Guy Kawasaki, "The 10/20/30 Rule of PowerPoint," December 30, 2005, www.guykawasaki.com/the_102030_rule

36. Tim Cook, Opening of the Apple Worldwide Developers Conference [WWDC], San Francisco, California, 2015, https://youtu.be/_p8AsQhaVKI?t=50s

37. Josh Berkus, "Give a Great Tech Talk" (presented at Linux Collab 2013, San Francisco, California, April 2013), www.slideshare.net/PGExperts/ggtt-linux-2013

38. Brené Brown, "The Power of Vulnerability" (presented at TED2010, Long Beach, California, June 2010), www.ted.com/talks/brene_brown_on_vulnerability

## Chapter 15: Promote Your Talk

39. Deploy 2010, www.xconomy.com/seattle/2010/04/29/deploy-2010-by-seattle-2-0

40. SlideShare, www.slideshare.net

41. Karen Catlin, "Turning Risk into Opportunity" (presented at NERCOMP's Unite and Ignite Your Career, Southbridge, Massachusetts, January 23, 2015), www.karencatlin.com/services/talks-panels/turning-risk-into-opportunity

42. Karen Catlin, "Measure Impact, Not Activity" (presented at Global Tech Women VOICES conference, March 12, 2014), www.karencatlin.com/measure-impact-not-activity

43. "Long-Form Posts on LinkedIn – Overview," https://help.linkedin.com/app/answers/detail/a_id/47445/~/long-form-posts-on-linkedin—overview

44. Medium, www.medium.com

## Intro to Part V: Special Talk Formats

45. Peter Cohan, Great Demo!: How to Create and Execute Stunning Software Demonstrations, 2nd ed. (Lincoln, NE: iUniverse, 2005), http://www.amazon.com/Great-Demo-Stunning-Software-Demonstrations/dp/059534559X

46. Oren Klaff, Pitch Anything: An Innovative Method for Presenting, Persuading, and Winning the Deal (Columbus, OH: McGraw-Hill Education, 2011), http://www.amazon.com/Pitch-Anything-Innovative-Presenting-Per-suading/dp/0071752854

## Chapter 16: Lightning Talks

47. Ignite, http://en.wikipedia.org/wiki/Ignite_(event)

48. PechaKucha, http://en.wikipedia.org/wiki/PechaKucha

49. Male Allies, www.maleallies.com

50. Renny Gleeson, "404, the Story of a Page Not Found" (presented at TED2012, Long Beach, California, February 2012), www.ted.com/talks/renny_gleeson_404_the_story_of_a_pag e_not_found

51. Margaret Gould Stewart, "How YouTube Thinks about Copyright" (presented at TED2010, Long Beach, California, February 2010), www.ted.com/talks/margaret_stewart_how_youtube_thinks _about_copyright

52. Chris Morris, "Technical Intimidation" (presented at RailsConf 2013, Portland, Oregon, April 2013), https://youtu.be/i4cryg-q_YM

## Chapter 17: Long-Form Talks

53. Karen Catlin, "Building Your Street Cred" (presented at Draper University, San Mateo, California, July 2013), https://youtu.be/xrKFhOL3rfA

54. Poornima Vijayashanker, "What Should Developers Do with Data?" (presented at FutureStack14, San Francisco, CA, October 2014), https://youtu.be/pDIT5ptJrvg

## Chapter 18: Panels

55. Lady Gaga, "Google Goes Gaga" (presented at Musicians at Google, Mountain View, California, March 22, 2011), https://youtu.be/hNa_-1d_0tA

56. Fresh Air, www.npr.org/programs/fresh-air

57. Cate Huston, "Panel Discussion and Dissent," www.catehuston.com/blog/2015/08/31/panel-discussions-and-dissent

58. Adam Quinton and Kara Swisher, "Investor Panel" (presented at Inspirefest 2015, Dublin, Ireland, June 2015), https://youtu.be/fo2dBENb1ss

59. "Women in Technology Panel" (presented at FedTalks 2014, Washington, DC, November 2014), https://youtu.be/IIysaY7_f4I

60. "How Women Are Engaging with Technology" (presented at Internet Week 2013, New York City, New York, May 2013), https://youtu.be/IOztlAUVg3M

## Chapter 19: Webinars and Podcasts

61. Google Hangouts On Air, http://plus.google.com/hangouts/onair

62. GoToWebinar, www.gotomeeting.com/webinar

63. Mike Curtis, "How to Record Skype, Google Hangouts, and Webinars," TechSmith Blog, October 18, 2012, http://blogs.techsmith.com/tips-how-tos/how-to-record-skype-google-hangouts-and-webinars

64. Camtasia, www.techsmith.com/camtasia.html

65. "Create a Survey Using Google Forms," www.support.google.com/docs/answer/87809?hl=en

66. Chatroll, www.chatroll.com

67. "Using Hashtags on Twitter," https://support.twitter.com/articles/49309

68. SoundCloud, www.soundcloud.com

69. iTunes podcasts, www.apple.com/itunes/podcasts

70. Rev, www.rev.com

## Attributions

6.1 Photo by Pauly Ting

6.2 Photo by Pauly Ting

6.3 Photo by Pauly Ting

6.4 Photo by Pauly Ting

10.1   http://www.audixusa.com/docs_12/units/HT2.shtml

10.2   http://www.rode.com/microphones/smartlav

10.3   Photo by Pauly Ting

10.4   Photo by Pauly Ting

11.1   https://en.wikipedia.org/wiki/Wright_brothers

11.2   Jake Hills https://unsplash.com/jakehills

11.3   Jake Hills https://unsplash.com/jakehills

11.4 Josh Berkus, "Give a Great Tech Talk" (presented at Linux Collab 2013, San Francisco, California, April 2013), www.slideshare.net/PGExperts/ggtt-linux-2013

11.5 Josh Berkus, "Give a Great Tech Talk" (presented at Linux Collab 2013, San Francisco, California, April 2013), www.slideshare.net/PGExperts/ggtt-linux-2013

11.6 Karen Catlin, "Turning Risk into Opportunity" (presented at NERCOMP's Unite and Ignite Your Career, Southbridge, Massachusetts, January 23, 2015), www.karencatlin.com/services/talks-panels/turning-risk-into-opportunity

RISK image on title slide: "Image courtesy of David Castillo Dominici, www.freedigitalphotos.net"

Tricycle image: "Image by bogwoppit, www.bigstock.com"

Seawall image: "Image used courtesy of Blue Square Thing on Flickr via Creative Commons License. 2012."

Made in the USA
San Bernardino, CA
15 April 2018